D1436742

STUDIES IN THE FOURTH GOSPEL

STUDIES IN THE FOURTH GOSPEL

Contributors

C. H. DODD
BARNABAS LINDARS
G. D. KILPATRICK
C. J. BARKER
T. H. L. PARKER
ERNEST EVANS
J. N. SANDERS
G. L. PHILLIPS
U. E. SIMON

Edited by F. L. CROSS

LONDON
A. R. MOWBRAY & Co. LIMITED

First published in 1957

PRINTED IN GREAT BRITAIN AT
THE UNIVERSITY PRESS
ABERDEEN

FOREWORD

THE Studies contained in this volume were originally written as a series of lectures for the Fourth Theology and Ministry Convention which met at Christ Church, Oxford, in September 1956 under the presidency of the Bishop of Oxford. They are in this respect a sequel to *Studies in Ephesians* issued by the same publisher a year ago.

The 'Problem of the Fourth Gospel', in its historical, theological and religious aspects alike, has never received more serious attention than in our own day and yet it remains with us, as provoking and challenging as ever. Readers of these pages will unite with the editor in gratitude to the authors for their stimulating contributions to a supremely great theme and for giving their ready consent to publication in the present form.

F. L. CROSS

Christ Church,
   Oxford.
September, 1957

CONTENTS

I

THE PROLOGUE TO THE FOURTH GOSPEL AND CHRISTIAN WORSHIP

by C. H. DODD, D.D.

WORSHIP may be defined, in respect of its central moment, as the acknowledgment by man of the glory of God. In Christian worship we acknowledge the glory of God in the person of Christ (ἐν προσώπῳ Χριστοῦ, II Cor. iv. 6).

Such worship is a response to the Gospel, which is defined as 'the Gospel of the glory of the blessed God' (I Tim. i. 11), or, which amounts to the same thing, 'the Gospel of the glory of Christ, who is the image of God' (II Cor. iv. 4).

The Gospel, then, declares to us the glory of God as it is revealed in Christ, and the only appropriate response to this Gospel is worship : 'Holy, holy, holy, Lord God of Hosts ; heaven and earth are full of thy glory. Glory be to thee, O Lord most high.'

The glory of God revealed in Christ is the theme of the Prologue to the Fourth Gospel. 'The Word became flesh, and we beheld His glory': that expression is intended as an epitome of what the Gospel has to say to us. It is written (by implication) over each of the episodes of which the story is composed. Not only in the 'beginning of signs' at Cana of Galilee (ii. 11), but in all His significant actions (σημεῖα), the incarnate Word 'manifested His glory'; and most of all in that final and inclusive 'sign' of the 'lifting up' of the Son of Man, in which God glorified His Son that the Son also might glorify Him (xiii. 31-32, xvii. 1).

In considering the Prologue, therefore, we have in our minds the *whole* story which it epitomizes and interprets. We are enquiring how the setting within which the incarnation of the Word is portrayed in these few momentous sentences illuminates the nature of Christian worship as a response to the Gospel.

First, we must examine the terms which the evangelist employs, and principally the term λόγος itself. That term brings together two distinct modes of human thought and experience, the Hellenic and the Hebraic. Both modes enter into Christian worship.

In Greek, λόγος connotes the principle of reason and order, wherever that principle is found to be at work— whether in the structure of the universe, or in the craftsman's deliberate design, or in logical thought, or in the considered speech of a rational being. I cannot doubt that in epitomizing the Gospel story in the terms, ὁ λόγος σὰρξ ἐγένετο, the evangelist was aware of this wealth of significance in the term he used—or, shall I say rather, he *felt* intuitively the weight of meaning with which it was charged for any Greek-thinking person. When he relates the healing of the blind or the feeding of the hungry multitude, still more when he relates the passion, death and resurrection of Christ, he wishes us to overhear the implication : in *this* action and in *that* it was the eternal λόγος that became flesh ; that is to say, that which there found expression in terms of human experience was the thought of the eternal Mind, the overriding design of the Master-craftsman, the ultimate structure of reality.

The appropriate response to such a Gospel is a λογικὴ λατρεία, a worship in which our rational part is concerned, answering to the rationality of the revelation. It is a worship that exercises our powers of thought and keeps them at stretch. This is not indeed a complete account of Christian worship ; for worship includes also a ' numinous '

element which, as Rudolf Otto taught us, cannot be completely rationalized. It is this element to which the word
' holy ' (*qadhosh*), as a liturgical term, properly corresponds.[1]
But no form of worship in which the *merely* numinous has
control can be a proper response to the glory revealed in
the λόγος : no such worship is fully or distinctively Christian.
    So much, then, for what we may call the Hellenic
hemisphere of thought and experience comprised in the
λόγος-idea. But in so far as the Greek term λόγος means
reasonable or considered *speech* it approaches the meaning
of the Hebrew term *dabhar*, ' word ', and is fittingly used
to translate it. Beyond this common area of meaning,
however, the denotation of the Hebrew term expands in a
different direction from the Greek. The other principal
meaning of *dabhar* is ' matter ', ' affair ', even ' event ' or
' act '. No such concrete meaning ever attaches to λόγος
in a properly Greek context ; but this concreteness is
integral to the Hebrew term. *Dabhar* as ' word ' is something actually spoken by way of communication from
person to person, on *this* occasion or on *that*. The word
of the Lord, we are told, came to such and such a prophet
in the *x*-th month, on the *x*-th day of the month, in the *x*-th
year of such and such a king of Israel. The speaking and
hearing of the word of God is a concrete, datable event :
at that time, at that place, God *spoke* to a man. The
attitude in which such an event places the man is expressed
in the form, ' Speak, Lord, for thy servant heareth '. The
Word demands attention and receptiveness. Thus, where
the Hebraic background of λόγος, as ' word ', is strongly
present, worship will have the form of colloquy between

---

[1] Paul was aware of this tension between the rational and the non-
rational elements in worship when he wrote, in the course of a passage
showing acute psychological observation (I Cor. xiv. 14-17), ' I will
pray τῷ πνεύματι ; I will pray also τῷ νοΐ. I will sing praises τῷ
πνεύματι ; I will also sing praises τῷ νοΐ.'

persons, in which the divine Interlocutor always initiates the conversation and the human interlocutor seeks to give the answer He requires.

That the Fourth Evangelist, aware as I believe him to have been of the Hellenic implications of the term λόγος, also felt in it the whole weight of the Hebrew-prophetic experience of 'hearing the word of the Lord', cannot be doubted. If in the person of Christ, in His words, actions and sufferings, was incarnate the principle of divine reason to which Greek thinkers bore witness, in Him also was incarnate the Word of the Lord that came to the prophets of Israel. The principle of reason, embodied, offers itself for contemplation—and thus John frequently uses the verb θεωρεῖν with Christ, or His actions, as object. On the other hand the Word of the Lord, embodied, offers itself to be heard and obeyed—and John constantly speaks of ' hearing ' and ' keeping ' the words of Christ (the λόγοι in which the one λόγος is uttered).

But whether λόγος as rational principle, or λόγος as word, is most prominent in any given context, it is always *as incarnate* that John finds the Λόγος to be the revelation of the eternal God. This means that we are concerned with something going far beyond a mere fusion of Hellenic and Hebraic ideas. Like Abt Vogler, who in his music made ' of three sounds not a fourth sound but a star ', John has made out of the two hemispheres of thought and experience, joined in a single term, a new category to comprehend a new and unique fact.

This fact is the career of a human person, whose earthly existence (his σάρξ) was an integral element in the history of mankind, continuous with that of all other men, having its particular *locus* in time and space, and subject to the incidents of mortality—hunger, thirst, fatigue ; joy, sorrow, conflict, pain and death—and yet a person in whose every act and word the divine λόγος found expression ; whose words were God's words, whose actions were ἔργα θεοῦ, to see whom was to see God with the eye of faith. It is the burden of the whole Gospel that at *every* point in the career of Jesus Christ this mystery of incarnation was present; and yet that it was concentrated with peculiar intensity in the climax of that career; in His death on the cross, which from one point of view was the final stage of His human humiliation, from the other point of view His ' lifting up ' to the pinnacle of divine glory.

From this it follows that Christian worship, which is the acknowledgement of the glory of God in the person of Jesus Christ, is orientated towards His incarnate life, and in particular towards His death on the cross. It begins with an ἀνάμνησις : we recall to mind, or commemorate, the Man who lived and died under Pontius Pilate. In particular, we ' declare ' (καταγγέλλομεν) His death. Christian worshippers are those (in Pauline phrase) οἷς κατ᾽ ὀφθαλμοὺς Ἰησοῦς Χριστὸς προεγράφη ἐσταυρωμένος (Gal. iii. 1)— ' before whose very eyes Jesus Christ has been " placarded " as crucified '. In the course of this ἀνάμνησις, we rehearse the very words, and repeat the actions, which Jesus Himself spoke and performed, ' the night on which He was betrayed ', viz. Thursday, Nisan 13, in the 17th year (or thereabouts) of the reign of Tiberius, Pontius Pilate being governor of Judaea. So concrete, so particular, is the event which brings us into the presence of the glory of God revealed.[1]

This ' remembrance ', ' declaration ' or ' placarding ' of the passion and death of the Lord brings with it the memory of His whole earthly career. No evangelist has insisted more emphatically than John upon the effective unity of the ministry of Jesus in word and deed with the ' lifting up ' of the Son of Man, as the revelation of the glory of God.

---

[1] This corresponds to the concreteness and particularity attached to the word of the Lord that came to the prophets, see above.

We are in line with his thought if in the presence of the memorials of the passion and death of the Lord we recall the incidents of His earthly life : His nativity, baptism and temptation, His works of mercy and power, His words of authority, and all that the Gospels relate of ' the days of His flesh '. Indeed the Prologue can be read, on one level of meaning, as a summary of the historical career of Jesus Christ : He, in whom was the light that brought life to men, entered into conflict with the forces of darkness, but (although they brought Him to the cross) the darkness never overwhelmed the light. He came to His own place, the Holy City of Jerusalem, and there Israel, His own people, rejected Him. Yet His coming was not in vain, for there were those who received Him, and in doing so were given the right to become children of God through faith in Him. And, the evangelist adds, with an eye upon the expanding church of his own day, ' out of His full store *all* of us have received grace upon grace, because, though no man has ever seen God, the only Son, the nearest to the Father's heart, made Him known '.[1] This is history, and all this is comprised in the καταγγελία which draws the Church to acknowledge the glory of God in worship.

But in these last sentences we have insensibly turned over the coin whose obverse is σάρξ, historical fact, and have looked at the reverse, which is λόγος, eternal meaning. For under the influence of this evangelist we find it impossible to contemplate the fact without discerning the meaning, just as for him the meaning became clear only in the presence of the fact—only when λόγος became σάρξ. We must now pursue the line of thought we have started on, and try to explicate more of the rich content of *meaning* lying within the Prologue as a summary of *facts*. At the

---

[1] Ἐξηγήσατο, a true aorist, referring to a single concrete event, viz. the event of Christ's coming, culminating in His passion and resurrection.

crucial point of the great argument—ὁ λόγος σάρξ ἐγένετο—
we may conceive ourselves (in view of what was said above)
as placed before the memorials of the passion and death of
the Lord, where worship begins. Here is the plain, concrete
witness to the σάρξ in which He came and which He gave
ὑπὲρ τῆς τοῦ κόσμου ζωῆς. But here also, says John, is the
Λόγος. I have already hinted at the wide ramifications of
the λόγος-idea in its Hellenic and Hebraic setting, and we
shall have to try to follow some of these further. But at this
point it is important to keep in mind the *order* of thought
in the evangelist's intention. In spite of a superficial resemblance to some Hellenistic teaching, what we have here is not
an attempt first to understand and define the nature of
deity (through the λόγος-idea) and then to employ the
concept thus arrived at as a formula for the deification, or
apotheosis, of a man. From a Hellenistic point of view the
climax of the argument, so regarded, would be sheer anti-
climax. For the aim of any such argument in a Hellenistic
writer would be to show how the eternal reality, after
being contaminated with matter in nature and in man, is
released from all such contamination and restored to purity
of essence. This is the proper and only climax. But in the
Prologue the λόγος relapses (as it would appear to a Hellenistic thinker) into matter (σάρξ) at the crucial point. But
for John this point really *is* crucial, in the sense that it is the
point from which alone we can truly discern and acknowledge the reality of the divine glory, whether in nature or
in human history.

If we take these two, nature and history, as corresponding
mainly to the Hellenistic and the Hebraic associations of the
term λόγος respectively, we shall have a serviceable, if over-
simplified, scheme for the examination of certain aspects
of the Prologue.

First, then, for the devout and thoughtful Greek, religious
emotion was chiefly excited by the contemplation of the order

and harmony of the universe. It is this principle of order and harmony that was chiefly in mind when he spoke of the λόγος as pervading the whole κόσμος. It is the principle by virtue of which it seemed possible (to Pythagoras as well as to modern physicists) to express the reality of the universe in mathematical equations. The spectacle of the heavenly bodies moving tranquilly for ever through their appointed orbits, unerringly, impersonally, awoke a sense of wonder which often passed into a religious awe. Where the λόγος in the universe was simply identified with God, this emotion took the form of an aspiration to be united with the κόσμος, or even of the experience of such unity, nobly expressed in Stoic writers such as Marcus Aurelius and Epictetus, or (in a somewhat different vein) the Hermetic writer who exclaims, ' Thou art whatever I am, thou art whatever I do, thou are whatever I say, for thou art all ! ' (Corpus Hermeticum, v. 11). Where a God beyond the κόσμος was postulated, He was apt to be defined by abstraction or negation, and religious emotion took the form of a craving for absorption into the Infinite. ' Make yourself to grow into immeasurable greatness, leap beyond all body, rise above all time, and become an eternal being (αἰών), and you will apprehend (νοήσεις) God ' (C.H. xi. 20).

These two forms of religious emotion—the craving for union with nature and the craving for the infinite beyond nature—are often taken to be ways of worship. We need not perhaps cavil about terms : ' cosmic emotion ' and the sentiment for the infinite may doubtless be in some sense religious attitudes ; they are pervaded with the sense of the ' numinous ' which can hardly be absent from any religious state of mind. But these are not what Christians mean by worship ; not, certainly, if we are to be guided by the traditional liturgies of the church, or, most certainly, if we are to be guided by the Prologue which is our present subject of study. Not, indeed, that the worshipping Church could, or should, be negligent of the glory of God as displayed in His works in nature. 'Heaven and earth are full of thy glory' : this is a universal and integral part of the Church's praise. In some of the ancient liturgies, as you will recall, the reference to God's works in creation is more explicit. Thus in the Liturgy of St. Mark we have, 'It is truly meet and right, pious and fitting, and profitable to our souls, O Thou self-existent, Master, Lord, God the Father almighty, that we should praise thee, hymn thee, make confession to thee night and day . . . to thee who madest heaven and all that therein is, earth and all that is in the earth, sea, fountains, rivers, lakes and all that is in them ; to thee who madest man in thine own image and likeness. . . .[1]

The Prologue itself begins, in a passage suffused with ' numinous ' feeling, by celebrating the divine transcendence and the creation of the universe and of man through the eternal light immanent in the whole (ἐν τῷ κόσμῳ ἦν). Yet it is not through contemplation of the eternal transcendence or of immanent deity that we behold the glory. The Λόγος became flesh ; and it was then, and there, and thus, that we ' beheld his glory, full of grace and truth'. Thus our worship embraces in its circumference the whole universe of being, with the eternal God as its source and its soul, but its centre is where ' grace and truth ' reached the decisive point of their manifestation, in the life and death of Christ. Thus union with God the Creator is not to be sought by denial of this world or of its human values in a mystical flight to an impersonal Absolute (καταφυγὴ πρὸς τὸ ὄν) ; nor is union with immanent deity to be sought by identification with nature, its processes and instincts. God and

---

[1] *The Primitive Liturgies*, ed. J. M. Neale, my translation. In the Liturgy of St. Clement the corresponding passage runs to more than two pages ! Cf. what was said by Father Gibbard at last year's meeting of this Convention, *Studies in Ephesians* (ed. F. L. Cross), pp. 117-118.

His glory are set before us in personal action, moral, beneficent, redemptive ; and in our response to this action we are to find such union with Him as God permits and desires.

In this way of approach to God, created things have a different value. They are no longer material encumbrances which we must shed in order to attain mystical union with the Absolute, nor yet themselves the objects of a romantic ' nature-mysticism '. They are sacramental signs of the God whom we know in Christ. Out of them we take those elements which He Himself chose for the purpose—bread and wine—as representing the whole natural order, the order of σάρξ in which He came, and comes, to us. As Christ offered His own σάρξ for the life of the world, so we are to offer, in fellowship with Him, not only the elements which we consecrate in church, but whatever elements of this material world we either contemplate or use—our own bodies, the food we eat, the light and beauty we enjoy, the natural forces we explore and manipulate. This offering is part of our λογικὴ λατρεία. In making it, we give our response to the glory of God in His works as seen through the incarnate Λόγος. This worshipful attitude to the Creator as known in His works I conceive to be the direct antithesis to that secular attitude which treats nature as something to be exploited for the glory of man.

We now turn to that part of the Prologue where the Hebraic associations of the term λόγος are nearest to the surface ; where we read that the λόγος ' came ', ' was received ' and ' gave ἐξουσία ', for all these are functions of the ' word of the Lord ' in the Old Testament. I suggested earlier that these verses could be read as an epitome of the historical career of Jesus Christ, and as such I believe the evangelist intended them to be read. But with his habit of thinking upon two levels of meaning I believe he also, and more directly, intended to recall the Old Testament

history, which turned upon the coming of the word of the
Lord through Moses and the prophets, its rejection by the
people at large (for where in the Old Testament will you
find a prophet to admit that Israel as a nation is loyal to the
Lord ?), and the raising up of a faithful ' remnant '. It is
significant that the evangelist, while describing this faithful
remnant as τέκνα θεοῦ, does not represent them (here at
any rate) as becoming such through a metaphysical process
analogous to physical generation (according to Hellenistic
doctrines of rebirth), but as being given the *right* (ἐξουσία)
to become τέκνα θεοῦ. 'Εξουσία is conferred by the ' word '
of a sovereign, who is the source of authority : here by the
' word ' of God, the Λόγος. Elsewhere the evangelist says
that it was those πρὸς οὓς ὁ λόγος τοῦ θεοῦ ἐγένετο (x. 35)
who were described by the Psalmist as ' gods and sons of
the Most High ' (Ps. lxxxii. 6). The reference to the
prophetic ' word of the Lord ' is unmistakable.

If, then, the light of the glory of God focused in the
Incarnation is from that point diffused over the whole of
created nature, so also it is diffused over the past history of
Israel. I have previously suggested that in the offering of
bread and wine we are acknowledging in the appointed
way the glory of God in His creation, apprehended and
understood in the Incarnate. We have now to observe that
in rehearsing and repeating historical words and actions by
way of ἀνάμνησις, καταγγελία, or προγραφή of an Event, we
necessarily associate ourselves with the whole historical
process which culminated in that Event. This determines
our understanding of the redemptive passion and death of
the Lord. Christ died for our sins κατὰ τὰς γραφάς : He
rose again the third day κατὰ τὰς γραφάς. To forget those con-
cluding last words is to lose the clue to the meaning both of
death and of resurrection (as it sometimes has been lost) ; to
remember them is to be committed to history. The ancient
liturgies bear witness to this by recalling the salient points of

Old Testament history. Thus, in the Liturgy of St. James :
' Him (fallen man) thou didst not overlook or forsake, but
didst discipline him like a merciful father ; didst call him
through the law ; didst educate him through the prophets ;
and afterwards didst send thine only Son, our Lord Jesus
Christ. . . .' The Liturgy of St. Clement rehearses (among
other things) the stories of Cain and Abel, Enoch and Noah,
Abraham and Lot, the Exodus and giving of the law, the
wanderings in the wilderness, and the conquest of Canaan,
before coming to the ἀνάμνησις of the incarnation, the
earthly life and ministry of Christ, His passion, death, resurrection and ascension. These are seen as the climax of the
Heilsgeschichte which runs all through the Old Testament.

Just as our worship includes the thankful acknowledgment of the glory of God in nature, so it includes also the
thankful acknowledgment of His wonderful works in
history. But just as nature can properly—or indeed safely
—become a means of approach to God only through the
incarnation of the λόγος which informs creation, so also
history is not in itself a safe guide to the understanding of
God's ways. It is history experienced from the Incarnation
as centre that bears witness to the glory of God, for in Christ
incarnate, crucified and risen, is disclosed and completed
the pattern imposed upon history by the Word of God :
a pattern, to put it briefly, of judgment and renewal, such
as is repeatedly exhibited in the prophetic history of Israel.

If, then, our worship is truly conditioned by the revelation of God in Christ the Word, it cannot avoid this
ordained pattern of judgment and renewal. Christian
worship does not begin with a surge of joyous or exalted
feeling which carries a man out of himself into regions of
spiritual bliss. It begins when in the presence of Christ
crucified we are placed under the judgment of God. ' Now
is the judgment of this world ', is the declaration which
John has placed over the scene of the crucifixion. It stands

over every ἀνάμνησις of the death of Christ.[1] And judgment must begin from the house of God (as we read in I Peter iv. 17, echoing the prophets). As we make our humble confession of sin, the judgment has begun, and as we proceed, the historical pattern fulfils itself afresh in us, for judgment is followed by renewal : the life of God is imparted to us through Christ risen from the dead. The way in which this pattern is worked out in traditional forms of liturgy I need not illustrate.

We thus come back to what is most simple and fundamental in the doctrine of the incarnate Word. Because the Lord is King, and His claim upon all His creatures is absolute, the word of God is first of all a call or command. Christ as λόγος is God's call to us, His command laid upon us. To worship God in Christ is not *primarily* to admire His works in nature and history, not even to praise His eternal wisdom and goodness ; it is to hear His call and obey His command. When Latin-speaking Christians gave to the central act of the Church's worship the name *sacramentum*, they seem to have heard in the word overtones of its other use for the soldier's oath of allegiance to his emperor. When Pliny wrote to Trajan that the Christians at their early morning service bound themselves by an oath (*se sacramento obstringere*) to commit no crime, it may be, as some commentators hold, that he was confusing the sacraments of Baptism and the Eucharist ; but these are in any case not so radically different but that the governor's attempt at labelling what he did not understand has hit upon an essential point. Unless our worship includes this element of whole-hearted allegiance, it has not reckoned with the full gravity of the statement : ' the *Word* became flesh '. This obedience to the Word of God is the ' living

[1] For the element of judgment in both Sacraments see C. F. D. Moule in *The Background of the New Testament and its Eschatology* (ed. W. D. Davies and D. Daube), pp. 464-481.

sacrifice' of ourselves, our souls and bodies, which is the required response to the full, perfect and sufficient sacrifice which Christ offered for us all.[1]

The basic statement, ὁ λόγος σὰρξ ἐγένετο, has been before us all through. We have turned it about and tried to see it in various aspects, so as in some measure to appreciate its relation to the statement which immediately follows : ἐθεασάμεθα τὴν δόξαν αὐτοῦ. We now recall that this statement is in turn followed by a descriptive clause : πλήρης χάριτος καὶ ἀληθείας. Grammarians discuss the question whether this clause is a description of the ' glory ' itself, or of Christ as manifesting the glory. For our present purpose it is not necessary to decide the question. The revelation of God's glory in the incarnate Word is πλήρης ἀληθείας, absolutely and finally real ; it is also πλήρης χάριτος, finally and absolutely beneficent. If we now take a broad view of the Gospel as a whole, with its picture of that absolute beneficence in action, we may arrive at what is perhaps an even more forcible way of putting the same thing. The life and death of Christ, as incarnate Λόγος, is seen to be the expression of ἀγάπη, the divine charity. It is this which is, in the last resort, the fullest manifestation of the glory of God which man is capable of receiving. The proposition ὁ λόγος σὰρξ ἐγένετο ramifies in many different directions in the Gospel, and various aspects of its meaning are brought out in numerous maxims which may be regarded as paraphrases of the fundamental statement. It is thus paraphrased most simply, in intimately personal terms, in the words : ' As the Father loved me, so have I loved you '. To this are added the words, ' Continue in my love '. This clause hints at the most profound and distinctive element of all in Christian worship.

[1] The obedience of Christ Himself is the fulfilment of all that sacrific e means ; see Heb. x. 8-10.

II

THE FOURTH GOSPEL
AN ACT OF CONTEMPLATION

by BARNABAS LINDARS, S.S.F.

THE choice of title for this paper is due to a conviction which came to me a few years ago when making the analysis which forms the substance of the following remarks. Trying to enter into the mind of John, I had the overwhelming impression that the figure of Christ was always there in his imagination, static and yet full of life, containing in himself the whole Gospel. So the reiterated ἐγώ εἰμι, I AM, is a theological concept in personal terms which holds the gaze of the contemplative. Dazzled and fascinated by this all-inclusive image, John knows that he is in the realm where truth passes beyond comprehension and defies intellectual description.

The occasion which induced John to write a gospel obviously cannot be recovered with certainty. His primary motive may have been to combat heresy, to strengthen the faithful, to bring the faith up to date with the shift in eschatological expectation, or simply to share his own experience. For whatever reason, John set out to write a gospel, but all the time this figure was before his eyes. All the time this figure is before our eyes as we read it.

We look to the end to see the *dénouement*. There we find the grand climax is contemplation of the risen, perfected and glorified Christ. The original composition, which did not include chapter xxi, ended with Thomas, and the readers of the gospel, gazing at Jesus in rapt adoration and saying ' My Lord and my God ! '

Now when I began my study of John, I was interested in the kind of approach which Dr. Austin Farrer had used in his *A Study in St. Mark* (1951). I was therefore expecting some kind of cyclic repetition of leading ideas and themes. I thus searched for this ending, this *dénouement*, not at the end of the book, but at the end of the first statement of the contents of the book. And there it was at the end of the Prologue : ' No man hath seen God at any time ; the only begotten Son, which is in the bosom of the Father, he hath declared him ' (i. 18).

This was a clue to suggest that the whole plan of the book can be deduced from the Prologue. i. 1-18 is the whole Gospel in miniature. It suggests that John is striving to present Christ to his readers in the fulness of his indescribable experience of him. The motive inevitably involves a highly artificial structure and arrangement of the available historical material. The selection of facts, the condensed reports of conversations, are geared into this one end with great dramatic skill.

The best method of describing something that is unknown is by contrast with what *is* known. This is a recurring feature of John's style. All the characters in the conversations are foils to our Lord. They take his words literally, but only so that he may show the real spiritual meaning. As soon as they have fulfilled their part they fade out of sight, as in the case of Nicodemus (ch. iii). We are left gazing at Jesus alone, and now know something more about him.

This method is evident from the very first words. The one definitive expression of religious truth known to the Jews is the Law. So John starts from there, giving a recapitulation of the first verses of Genesis.

But when John repeats the *beré'shîth* (In the beginning ...) his mind is, as always, filled with the image of Christ in all his perfection and beauty. The whole of what he has to say is already there, contained in the beginning. This is not to say that he did not intend to write a straightforward narrative. An author must have some scheme in mind when he begins to write. There are indications that John had a historical sequence in his mind, using the Jewish festivals as framework. But as he actually puts pen to paper the whole scheme falls into comparative insignificance because of a most important factor he had not reckoned with—the workings of his own mind. For narrative requires a steady movement from beginning to end, as in Mark. But in fact John's mind keeps reverting to the one beginning which contains the whole, so that every time he begins a new section he, as it were, starts all over again, though every time more and more can be taken for granted, and so a fuller and fuller picture is built up.

This is remarkably true to the special genius of Hebraic thought. As J. Pedersen has shown, the whole is contained in the beginning, the seed contains the whole tree, the first man Adam contains the whole human race, Abraham has in his loins the whole people of God. This is true of Semitic language structure also. The verbal idea is stated first, subject and object normally follow, and then any further development. So the whole Gospel grows out of the Prologue, and the Prologue itself grows out of its own opening statements. The growth is like a flower opening and revealing more and more of its beauty and glory, till the whole is revealed.

It is now time to attempt to show this by examining the Prologue in some detail.

i. 1-5. In the first five verses John works over Gen. i. 1-5. I would suggest that the Word (Logos) is identified not only with the act of creation ' when God spake and it was done ', but also with the ' spirit of God ' that ' was brooding upon the face of the waters '. But in this case John uses the word ' life ' rather than ' spirit ', and indeed throughout the Gospel ' spirit ' and ' life ' (in the sense of eternal life, life in or with God) are very closely linked. Then also the Word is ' light ', which is defined as something that is *within* man, and therefore implies knowledge or experience of God. Finally the Word, Life and Light are set in the widest possible context of the cosmic struggle, for the light in the darkness corresponds to the taming of the primeval chaos in Gen. i. 2. Thus in these first five verses we can already see a summary of the plot of the whole book, the struggle of the Incarnate Word with the powers of darkness.

i. 6–8. After this there is a sudden jolt. Why introduce the actuality of St. John the Baptist into the midst of the philosophical exposition ? It is because it is essential to John's purpose to insist all the time on the interaction of the philosophical and mystical with the actual and personal. As he already has decided to keep the plot moving by means of noting the reactions of men at each stage in the progress of thought, he follows this first adumbration of the plot by the fact of the Baptist's witness. At the same time the particularity of naming John the Baptist cannot be simply due to his subsequent importance in the earlier chapters, but also implies his special position as a representative—as the best representative—of those in whom ' the life was the light of men ', the Word indwelling and supernaturally moulding those who are not overcome by darkness ; for John the Baptist is the prophet par excellence, the truest mouthpiece of God short of the life itself.

i. 9–13. This leads into the first example of John's cyclic repetition. Verses 9–13, the rejection or reception of the Light, repeat in a fuller form the meaning of verses 4–5, the struggle of light and darkness. This anticipates a recurring characteristic of the Gospel. Each section has what one may call a ' Witness ' subdivision, which often mentions the Baptist by name. In each case this is the opportunity to

note that some people rejected our Lord's teaching, whereas
' many believed ', or ' the disciples believed '.

The positive aspect of this brings the thought back to
the beginning again : the purpose of the activity of the
Word is to bring men into the life of the eternal Word in
God. This is only possible by the work of God himself.
It cannot be achieved by human nature (blood, i.e. physical
descent), nor by emotion (the will of the flesh), nor by
will-power (the will of man). Man cannot gain his end by
any property of his own nature as man, nor by wishing
for it with all his soul, nor by any practical steps which his
own mind and reason may suggest, because man is not
equal with God. Only God himself can raise man to sonship.

i. 14. It is now inevitable that John should state what
he has all the time been leading up to, in terms derived from
this last thought. The Word has now been united with
humanity precisely in the manner which has just been
described as impossible in human nature as such. Here is
the One who was literally born not of blood (human
generation), nor of human desire, nor of human volition.
Yet he is become truly human, fully and perfectly. He is
' full of grace and truth '. And so through his human flesh
he reveals in a manner accessible to human eyes the invisible
glory of God, whom no one can look upon and live.

i. 15-17. The remainder of the Prologue goes back once
more over the Witness motif. First the Baptist witnesses
to the Word made flesh. Then those who receive him
acknowledge that the grace which they share is not derived
from anything in themselves but comes from him. It is
his indwelling which has caused this grace, not their efforts
to keep the Law.

Apparently nothing has prepared us for this sudden
mention of Moses and the Law. But it was of course
present in John's mind all along, for it is his starting-point.
It is the reason why he has begun his Gospel with *berē'shîth*.

He was bound to mention it explicitly sooner or later. He has referred to it mentally in verse 14, when he chose to describe the Incarnation in terms of the Tabernacle, and of the Sinai theophany when the Law was given. The Law, being an accommodation to man's frail human nature, is an act of grace, but not a *living principle* such as is now revealed and made available ; it is also the truth of God, but only partial—not the *perfect glory* made apprehensible in its entirety.

i. 18. From this the Prologue comes naturally to its conclusion by reasserting the Incarnation of the Word in reverse manner : not the Word being made flesh, but the flesh, the human person, being the Word, uttering, declaring, interpreting the Father from the depths of the Divine Being.

May I briefly summarize this exposition of the Prologue by drawing attention to its three basic literary elements ? It contains a theological statement of the Word, Life and Light ; the Sign of the Word in the announcement of the Incarnation ; and the Witness to it in terms of John the Baptist and the response (acceptance or rejection) by mankind.

It remains now to give a very rapid survey of the main structure of the whole Gospel to show how the cyclic repetition progressively deepens the truth stated in the Prologue. Each main section contains material which may be designated by the three elements observed in the Prologue : Theological Statement, Sign and Witness. But the self-developing exposition makes the structure very much more complex than a simple summary such as this can show. Every section picks up the old themes at the same time as it introduces new ones to be worked out later. As the work proceeds the cross-references back to the Prologue and to preceding sections become more and more intricate. The whole thing gathers momentum and comprehensiveness simultaneously, like a snowball rolling down a steep hill. This can be worked out by collecting the occurrences of significant theological words and noting the pattern they produce. Nevertheless a complete analysis shows that the complexity obscures the basic structure without destroying it. If therefore the following brief survey appears to be a gross over-simplification, it should be remembered that it is based on a very detailed analysis which has taken the complexity into account.

i. 1-ii. 12. The first main section consists of i. 1-ii. 12. You will notice at once that it contains within itself the Prologue which we have already studied. It is in fact a perfect illustration of the cyclic structure of the whole.

The *whole* of the Prologue, i. 1-18, is the Theological Statement. The rest of chapter i is the Witness, and the marriage at Cana is the Sign. Again we have the Gospel within the Gospel, for it contains the coming of Christ, his mystical death as the Passover Lamb, and the inauguration of the kingdom, the marriage feast of the Lamb. But this is superimposed on a simple historical purpose—to set the stage for the narrative-plot, introducing Jesus as a historical person, with his friends and his *Sitz im Leben*. We notice that Jesus is never called the Logos after the statement of i. 14, σὰρξ ἐγένετο. John substitutes the Son (i.e. of God), so as to preserve the fully personal idea throughout. In this section, then, we are contemplating Christ, and the picture adumbrated in the Prologue is filled out in the remainder of the section by the great sense that he is here, the Coming One, and behold all things are made new.

ii. 13-iii. 36. We pass on to the second main section, ii. 13-iii. 36. The order of structural elements is reversed, with the Sign first, as in fact is more usual. The Sign is the cleansing of the temple, the Statement is the conversation with Nicodemus, and the Witness is the Baptist's humble willingness to decrease that Christ may increase. We find in this section the themes of the Prologue—the temple of the flesh of the Word of God, the life that is the Spirit, and the light which struggles with darkness. The new facet in the total picture is the assertion that the Son has been sent by the Father to give eternal life to those who believe, a thing which is new and distinct from the Law of Moses (represented by the Jewish temple and the Jewish ruler), though the true fulfilment of it.

iv. 1-54. Chapter iv continues the same plan and deepens the truth just given still further. The Statement is the conversation with the woman of Samaria, the Witness is the reaction of the Samaritans and of the Galileans, and the Sign is the healing of the nobleman's son. This section develops the description of the new grace given by Christ in terms of living water, but also shows that this is to be appropriated by an act of personal belief in the Figure who stands before the woman of Samaria, and stands before the eyes of the contemplative soul. The Sign of the nobleman's son puts this belief and its healing result into action.

v. 1-47. But what is the authority for ascribing this spiritual power to the Word made flesh? The next main section deals with this question, and shows it to be a self-authenticating power, needing no testimony from man. The Sign is the healing of the paralytic ; the Statement is a discourse on judgment and resurrection ; and this runs on into a comparison of the reactions to John the Baptist and to Moses, which form the Witness.

vi. 1-71. The great chapter vi brings all this to a climax by expounding the actual nature of this new, spiritual, self-authenticating power, which may be appropriated only by personal response to Jesus himself. It is the mystery of mutual indwelling of God and man, presented in the Sign of the feeding of the multitude ; the Statement of the Bread of Life and of the Flesh and Blood which must be consumed ; and the Witness of the many who went back and of the twelve who, led by Peter, asserted ' Thou hast the words of eternal life '.

So we have come to the end of the story once more. Another Gospel within the Gospel has been completed, this time not i. 1-18, nor i. 1-ii. 12, but i. 1-vi. 71, and this is the minor climax of the whole structure.

All that has been said so far in this rapid survey may be gathered under the heading ' grace '. But Christ is ' full of grace and truth ', and the next section begins the exposition of Christ the Truth in terms of the Light of the World. The horizon widens. Though superficially we are still occupied with the unbelieving Jews, the underlying plan is no longer the contrast between Law and Grace (or letter and spirit, to use Pauline terminology), which is linked to the Judaistic controversy. Now the underlying plan is universal in scope. It concerns the light that lighteneth *every* man. We may call it the universal experience of conscience, though that is a dangerous limitation of the light idea in John. Call it rather the Logos of the Stoics, defined in terms of the Johannine Prologue, and not the other way round.

vii. 1-52. At any rate chapter vii sets the stage for this new development. It repeats many themes already given in previous sections—the Law, the temple, the living water—but adds a new note : The forces of evil desire to kill Jesus ; the struggle is coming out into the open. The theme of judgment has only been hinted at before ; now it is a burning issue. The Christ whom we contemplate is a sharp sword, piercing to the soul and to the marrow.

viii. 12-59. I omit the pericope vii. 53-viii. 11, for viii. 12 continues the controversy without a break. Though no prophet is expected to arise out of Galilee, yet it is from Galilee of the Nations that the light has arisen upon the people who sat in darkness (Is. ix. 1-2). Gazing at the

Christ of the seed of David we see in him the Light of the World. Just as in the discussion on grace the question of authority had to be settled first, and the solution of self-authenticating saving activity was given in chapter v, so now the claim to be the Light of the World is authenticated by Jesus' assertion of his direct procession from God himself. There the contrast was with Moses, the giver of the Law ; here the contrast is with Abraham, the father of the people of God. ' Before Abraham was, I AM.' ' In the beginning was the Word, and the Word was with God, and the Word was God.'

ix. 1-41. After these preliminaries chapter ix has the normal structure of the Sign of the man born blind ; the Statement, which in this case is the cross-examination of the man himself and not of Jesus ; and the Witness, which contrasts the man's simple belief and worship of Jesus with the blindness and obstinacy of the Jews. We now know that to worship the Figure whom we contemplate is the means of regaining our true sight, so that the light may shine in us.

x. 1-42. The nature of this restored sight is given in the next chapter. It turns out to be relationship, described in the parable of the sheep and the shepherd. The parable seems to take the place of a Sign. It is followed by a State-ment of the eternal safety of the sheep on the basis of the mutual indwelling of the Father and the Son ; and ends with a brief Witness asserting that ' many believed '. The quality of this relationship is defined in terms of sacrifice : ' I lay down my life for the sheep.' The interlocking of all the previous themes suggests thoughts too numerous to mention. We may notice, for instance, that the date is the feast of the dedication and that Jesus is in the temple, two reminders that he is himself the holy place, because the Word was made flesh. When he ' makes himself equal with God ' he is simply saying openly what had been said by John in the very first phrases of the whole book. We have here reached a point parallel to the long Bread of Life teaching in chapter vi. There the power of grace was described in terms of mutual indwelling. Here the light of truth is disclosed in terms of mystical unity.

But there is more than a parallel here. There is the answer to a question raised in chapter vi and left on one side : ' How can this man give us his flesh to eat ? ' The answer is adumbrated in the forecast of his sacrifice which Jesus gives in this chapter on the sheep and shepherd. Here is an important new element in the picture, which shows how the teaching on light in chapters vii-x, as it were, scoops up all the previous teaching, so that this fourth Gospel within the Gospel must again be regarded as beginning at chapter i and extending right through the first ten chapters.

xi. 1-57. In fact it must be extended to include chapter xi as well. The Bread of Life chapter was a minor climax. Chapter x is weak by comparison from the literary point of view. But the structural balance is perfectly maintained, because the grand description of the raising of Lazarus forms a fitting climax to this section and to all that has gone before. The Sign of the miracle of resurrection and the Statement of the resurrection and the life are completely interlocked, but the chapter ends characteristically with a Witness section, concerned with the almost complete rejection of our Lord, who has now revealed grace and truth fully. The skill with which all the themes are drawn together is masterly. The death of Lazarus is the test case for the struggle of light against darkness (verse 10). It is the means for the revelation of the glory of God (verse 40). It is effected by the creative word, ' Lazarus, come forth '. It is a new creation, for by ordinary physical processes the body has already begun to decay. The result is a prefiguring of the risen Christ himself, anticipating many important details of the resurrection narrative—the tomb, the stone, the grave-clothes. It thus forms a bridge between the ministry of our Lord and his own Passion and Resurrection. It is the last Little Gospel, for the next climax will be the completion of the whole book.

So the cyclic structure reaches its final expression. i. 1-18 led up to the statement of the only-begotten Son declaring the Father. i. 1-ii. 12 led up to the marriage-supper of the Lamb in the wedding at Cana. i. 1-vi. 71 led up to the Bread of Life and Peter's confession of belief. i. 1-xi. 57 has led up to the resurrection of Lazarus. i. 1-xx. 31 leads up to the resurrection of Christ and Thomas's cry ' My Lord and my God ! '

xii. 1-xiii. 38. From chapter xii onwards the whole narrative is fastened on the person of Christ. The original structure is abandoned and the Passion narrative takes control. It is Christ who is the focal point in the cosmic struggle. It is no accident that xii. 35 uses the same Greek word $\kappa\alpha\tau\alpha\lambda\acute{\alpha}\beta\eta$ as i. 5 $\kappa\alpha\tau\acute{\epsilon}\lambda\alpha\beta\epsilon\nu$: the darkness comprehended it not. The sense of the universal significance of the drama hangs heavily over chapter xiii, which adds a new dimension to the previous picture of the Christ. The Christ who is full of grace and truth, who is the Bread of Life and the Light of the World and the Resurrection, whose active power consists in indwelling in the faithful, and whose enlightening presence consists in mystical union with the faithful, can sum all this up in the new commandment to love one another.

The long ' discourses ' that follow do not break the flow of the narrative. From the literary point of view they provide the necessary fulness, because we have seen that each revolution of the cyclic structure is extended to a larger and larger compass. This corresponds with the need to gather up the previous ideas with greater and greater comprehensiveness. What has been done at the Supper in chapter xiii is now expounded in terms of thoroughgoing identification of our Lord and the disciples, all and each reproducing his life on the two levels of the individual and of the whole church. This in its turn is only reproducing the essential meaning of his own relation with the Father. The great prayer of chapter xvii focuses attention on this, and so deftly brings the reader back to the narrative of the Passion, the definitive Sign of divine glory.

Finally chapter xx, using available historical material, presents Christ in the glory which has been present in the mind of John all the way through. The empty tomb leads up to a statement of the beloved disciple's intelligent perception and belief. Mary Magdalene sees Jesus ready for the glory of the Ascension. The disciples see the scars of the Passion and are commissioned to continue the redeeming work. Thomas stops short at the glorious scars, and the book, as originally planned, ends with his adoration and the challenge to all readers to believe.

The reader is bound to be left gazing with Thomas. Before his eyes there has been presented a pregnant multiplicity in unity which fascinates the contemplative. To read John is an act of contemplation ; it is to share in John's own act of contemplation. This act is itself the means of appropriating the fulness of grace and truth, as the Rev. G. L. Phillips' paper on ' Faith and Vision ' clearly shows. John has communicated the incommunicable, and the secret of the entire universe has been made known in a Person who is victorious love.

THE RELIGIOUS BACKGROUND
OF THE FOURTH GOSPEL

by G. D. KILPATRICK, D.D.

A N older friend once said to me : 'If I were not con-
vinced that the Apostle wrote the Gospel according to
St. John, I would lose my faith.' This remark surprises us
today. It shows how deeply a previous generation was
concerned about the authorship of the Gospel and how
much our interest has turned away from such enquiries.
Nowadays we are much more concerned about the interpretation of the book, as indeed of the New Testament
books as a whole.

We quickly discover that the more we are interested in
the interpretation of the Gospel the more we have to concern ourselves with its background. An example of this
concern is to be found in Dr. C. H. Dodd's *Interpretation
of the Fourth Gospel* (1953), where the discussion of the
background of the Gospel comes at the beginning of the
book and provides the key to much that follows.

Why is the background so significant ? The first verses
of the Gospel point to an answer. Here we encounter the
term λόγος. We refer it to Jesus, but what does the
evangelist mean by so describing Him ? At once we begin
to look elsewhere to find how the word was used in the
evangelist's day and in the immediately preceding centuries.
We examine the Septuagint, Philo, the Greek philosophers
and religious writers. To which of these was the evangelist
most indebted for the ideas with which he worked and for
the term he used ? We find λόγος employed with a

considerable range of meaning in these various sources, much of it relevant to the use of the term in St. John.

What are the conclusions to which scholars have come about this background ? We soon discover that they are not all of one mind and that at different periods of the enquiry different fashions prevailed. Thus toward the beginning of the century it was customary to find an important element in the background of St. John in Philo, and to him scholars turned for light on the words and ideas of the Gospel.

We are no longer ready today to regard Philo as being the source of the distinctive ideas of the Evangelist. Obviously the thought of each is related to that of the other and Philo can be used to illuminate the Gospel, but there are clear and marked distinctions which the discussions have pointed out. For example, Philo's religious thought, even when it is dealing with a term like λόγος, does not present a religion of incarnation ; the Gospel obviously does. Philo again is demonstrably drawing on Greek philosophy to provide the forms and ideas he uses to expound his views. No such similar debt to Greek philosophy can be found in our Gospel. The result of this can be seen in our commentaries. Philo is still quoted and is of great service to the interpreter, but the exposition is no longer dominated by him.

If the background of the Gospel is not Philo, where can it be found ? Repeated attempts have been made to provide this background from Gnosticism. Reitzenstein was a pioneer in this line of interpretation. It dominates much of Bultmann's commentary on the Gospel. In particular the Mandaean documents were used as a source of Gnostic ideas such as were thought to have influenced John. To this end they are frequently quoted in the second edition of Bauer's commentary on the Gospel. An adequate and telling discussion of theories of a dominant Gnostic background is to be found in a paper by Dr. R. P. Casey, *Gnosis, Gnosticism and the New Testament*.[1] The comments of the scholars cited by Dr. Casey can only be regarded as decisive.

Another endeavour finds the background of the Gospel in that collection of tracts called the *Hermetica*. The *Hermetica* range from perhaps the first to third centuries A.D., and give an interesting picture of some aspects of the religion of the time. We are fortunate in having a good edition of these texts in the Budé series with a French translation. Scott's large edition deals rashly with the texts, but, in addition to a wealth of material in the commentary and introduction, it has a very useful index. Reitzenstein played an important part in bringing these texts to the notice of scholars.

Professor C. H. Dodd has done a great deal in this country to draw attention to the *Hermetica*. Over twenty years ago he published interesting studies of them in the second half of his book, *The Bible and the Greeks* (1935). In his recent book, *The Interpretation of the Fourth Gospel*, he draws largely, though not exclusively, on them for the understanding of John. Again, as with Philo, there are obvious resemblances in ideas and the words used to express them, and many scholars have gladly followed Professor Dodd in using the *Hermetica* as one of the main tools of interpretation.

Despite the interest of these texts there are reasons for a certain reserve over their application to the interpretation of our Gospel. It is surprising, for example, that to understand this book we are asked to turn so often to the religious and philosophical ideas of contemporary paganism rather than to the Bible and first-century Judaism. That that suggestion is surprising is no reason for thinking it wrong, nor yet for excepting it from examination.

[1] In *The Background of the New Testament and its Eschatology. Studies in Honour of C. H. Dodd*, pp. 52-80.

How are we to determine the place of the *Hermetica* as compared with the Bible in the background of the Gospel ? There is one possible line of enquiry which has still to be adequately explored. St. John and the *Hermetica* existed in Greek and the Septuagint was the Bible for Greek-speaking Christians at the time when the Evangelist wrote. This suggests that we compare the vocabularies of these texts. Such a comparison would not settle the matter but would provide a strong indication in which direction to look for the interpretation of John.

First, let us examine a few important terms from texts such as the *Hermetica* which have already penetrated into Hellenistic Judaism, to see how far they appear in the Gospel. Secondly, let us compare the three vocabularies in bulk to see if we can draw any conclusions from such a comparison.

The emphasis on Gnosticism among some commentators suggests that we look at γνῶσις itself. It occurs, of course, in pagan texts including the *Hermetica* and also in the LXX, Philo, Josephus, other New Testament writers, I Clement and Ignatius, but not in John. We must not, however, make too much of this as the verb γινώσκειν is used several times by the Evangelist.

Another word which may serve as an indication of the degree to which Greek paganism has penetrated Hellenistic Judaism and early Christianity is μυστήριον. It describes certain religious rites first in the Greek world and then in the Graeco-Roman world. Yet it makes its way into the Septuagint, being found in Wisdom. It also appears in the *Prayer of Asenath*, a Hellenistic Jewish text of perhaps the first century B.C. In the New Testament, it occurs in the Epistles and once in each of the Synoptic Gospels. It is found in Philo and Josephus and Ignatius and of course in the *Hermetica*. It is lacking, however, in John.

'Αθανασία is associated with a view of human continuity

which is essentially Greek, the immortality of the soul. Over against it stands the Hebraic idea of the resurrection of the body. Yet ἀθανασία has begun to find its way into Judaism. Wisdom, IV Maccabees, the *Prayer of Asenath*, Philo, Josephus all have it or the kindred ἀθάνατος. The noun is at I Cor. xv. 53 f., I Tim. vi. 16. Both words occur in the Apostolic Fathers, neither in John.

Δημιουργός and its derivatives have a history in Greek philosophical and religious speculation. They appear frequently in the *Hermetica*, being used, for example, of God and the Logos. In Philo, God is described as creator as δημιουργός and the word occurs in this sense in Heb. xi. 10, frequently in I Clement, in Symmachus' version of Job xxxvii. 15, xxxviii. 4 and in Diognetus. They are not to be found in John.

The absence of these words, γνῶσις, μυστήριον, ἀθανασία and δημιουργός, from our Gospel suggests that it is not as dependent on the *Hermetica* as we might suppose. A rapid perusal of Ferguson's index in Scott's edition reveals other significant terms in the *Hermetica* which are absent from John. Thus the results of our first examination of some important terms in the *Hermetica* are unfavourable to the view which sees these texts as part of the background of the Gospel.

We have now to compare the vocabulary of John with that of the Greek Bible and that of the *Hermetica*. For this comparison I have taken words of the first four letters, α-δ, and have omitted proper names, prepositions, particles and other grammatical words. For these letters I have listed 197 words in John. Eighty-two of them are common to John and the *Hermetica* and 115 are absent from these texts. Thus just over two-fifths of this part of John's vocabulary occurs in the *Hermetica* also, not a large proportion, if the *Hermetica* occupied an important place in the background of the Fourth Gospel.

When we turn to the comparison with the Septuagint the results are different. Of John's 197 words only eight fail to reappear in the Septuagint, roughly one in twenty-five. For this count only the Septuagint proper has been consulted. The later translations and texts like the *Psalms of Solomon* have been ignored.

Let us examine the eight Johannine words that are not in the Septuagint : ἀνθρωποκτόνος, viii. 44, ἄντλημα, iv. 11, ἀποσυνάγωγος, ix, 22, xii. 42, xvi. 2, ἄρραφος, xix. 23, ἀρχιτρίκλινος, ii. 8, 9(2), δαιμονίζεσθαι, x. 21, δηνάριον, vi. 7, xii. 5, διακονεῖν, xii. 2, 26(2). Two of these, ἀποσυνάγωγος and δηνάριον, would be an anachronism in the Septuagint. Four, ἀνθρωποκτόνος, ἄντλημα, ἄρραφος, δαιμονίζεσθαι, occur only once in John and cannot be regarded as vital to his religious thought. The two remaining terms, ἀρχιτρίκλινος and διακονεῖν likewise do not indicate religious differences.

We may conclude that in all essentials the vocabulary of John and the Septuagint are identical for α-δ. This identity stands in marked contrast to the relation of this part of John's vocabulary in the *Hermetica*. With the *Hermetica* John's vocabulary has surprisingly little contact if they share a common religious outlook.

In accepting this conclusion we must recognize that it lies under two limitations. First we have examined only a sample, the letters α-δ, and, while there is no reason to think that an examination of the whole vocabulary would yield materially different results, we must recognize that the comparisons must be made for the whole vocabulary, if all results are to be firmly established. Secondly, our argument is largely one of statistics and we cannot expect to settle the matter on a word-count, even if it is supplemented by the scrutiny of a few terms. For an exact estimate we must weigh our words as well as count them.

Subject to these limitations our preliminary test of

vocabulary suggests quite clearly that John and the *Hermetica* are not closely related, but that John and the Septuagint are. Before this suggestion can be regarded as established other considerations, of history and thought for example, must be taken into account.

One consideration in particular must weigh with us. It behoves us to speak cautiously about the reasons why the Jews translated their Scripture into Greek. It is clear, however, that this translation is the principal monument of a migration, the migration of a religion and theology from one language to another. It must be recognized that in making this migration Judaism underwent the influence of the Greek language and the Greek world. This influence was, however, less than the effect of the Jewish Scriptures on the Greek language. It was in effect the creation of a new religious vocabulary in Greek.

Later we find evidence that, in addition to acclimatizing itself in the Greek world, Judaism began to seek to make converts of its pagan members. We have the remains of a missionary literature in such works as the *Prayer of Asenath* and the *Sibylline Oracles*. It is not surprising if in presenting Judaism to the pagan Hellenistic world these works make some use of the language of Hellenistic religion. The *Prayer of Asenath* seems to have gone further in this direction than the Fourth Gospel.

Whatever his purpose Philo seems to have proceeded in a similar way. He makes use of the language of Greek thought to present the Judaism of the Septuagint. He also shows himself acquainted with the language and ideas of Hellenistic paganism. While he is a valuable aid toward understanding John, for example in his use of the term λόγος, he is much more permeated by pagan thought and language.

It is against this background that we must see the Fourth Gospel. Its purpose too is a matter for dispute. Was it a missionary document directed to the world, or was it written for the Church? Both views have been maintained.

On either view John presents the Christian revelation in terms of the Biblical religion in Greek. The Greek vocabulary for such presentation had already been created, as we have seen, by Hellenistic Judaism, principally in the Septuagint. Like the Septuagint John constitutes part of a movement of Biblical and Jewish religion into the Greek world. In view of this it is not surprising if the language of the Fourth Gospel is, with little exception, the language of the Septuagint.

This general consideration reinforces the conclusion drawn from our partial examination of Johannine vocabulary. The language of the Gospel is the language of the Greek Bible just as the main element in the background of the Gospel is the Biblical religion. Further, John represents a stage in the invasion of Hellenistic paganism by Judaism and, later, by Christianity, and not an invasion of the Biblical religion by the pagan world.

If this picture is true, the *Hermetica* are no proper part of John. This is supported by one consideration of detail. In our examination of the vocabulary of John there was no word common to John and the *Hermetica* which did not recur in the Septuagint. Likewise it is doubtful whether there is any significant element in the Gospel which it shares only with the *Hermetica*. If we conclude rightly, we can discard the *Hermetica* along with the Mandaean texts and other evidences of Gnosticism. They constitute no significant part of the background of the Gospel, they do not provide the key to its interpretation.

The Evangelist presents the revelation of Jesus Christ as the fulfilment of the Biblical religion.[1] The making of the

---

[1] Cf. H. Riesenfeld, in *The Background of the New Testament and its Eschatology*, 81–95, ' The Mythological Background of New Testament Christology', especially p. 81.

Greek Bible had created the Greek vocabulary for such a presentation in the Hellenistic world. Hellenistic elements have penetrated only in so far as they have already been assimilated in Hellenistic Judaism. Such is the religious background that our limited enquiry suggests for the Fourth Gospel.

IV

REPENTANCE AND THE NEW BIRTH

by C. J. BARKER, M.A.

IT is somewhat startling to reflect that neither in the Fourth
Gospel nor in the Johannine Epistles is there any mention
of repentance. The Synoptists record that Jesus began His
ministry bidding men to repent and believe the Gospel. In
that He followed up and completed the message of His
forerunner, and stood in the line of the Hebrew prophets.
The ground of His summons was that the Kingdom of
Heaven was at hand. Then comes a variety of teaching
and activity to declare and illustrate the nature and structure
of the Kingdom. We are left with the unmistakable impression that repentance is the gateway into the Christian life.

In the conversation with Nicodemus Jesus lays it down
that a man can neither see nor enter the Kingdom unless
he has first been born anew. This stands in the Fourth
Gospel as the unequivocal declaration how the new life
begins.

The contrast between the Synoptists and St. John on this
point confronts us with a matter of urgency and practical
concern as those entrusted with the Kerygma. Probably
often enough we have said to ourselves, and heard it in
discussions, that if only we could present with sufficient
clarity and persuasiveness the vision of the Kingdom men
would press into it, and we should be moving towards the
conversion of England. Much of the advocated technique
of evangelization is based on the assumption that the prime
need is to kindle the imagination.

But now, it would seem, the Fourth Gospel declares that
unless men are already born anew they cannot see this that

we are so anxious to depict : we may only be showing
pictures to the blind ! The decisive work has to be done
before we go into action.

At this point we must notice that birth *may* be a metaphor.
In dealing with truth presented in metaphor we are faced
with the difficulty of steering between Scylla and Charybdis.
Either we force the metaphor to carry more than it can
bear, by articulating and stressing every detail, or we risk
evacuating it of some of its essential teaching, and really
fail to take the metaphor seriously.

There are two facts about ' birth ' which cannot escape
our attention.

(i) Birth is an involuntary event. We were never consulted about being born ; we never gave our consent to
coming into this world. Birth is certainly no act of the
individual's will.

(ii) Birth settles the capacities and propensities with
which we enter upon life. We were born human beings,
thus involved in all that being human entails. It is only
subsequently that we have to face the responsibility for the
use or misuse, the developing or the stifling, of our innate
potentialities.

The contrast with ' repentance ' as a starting-point is complete. Repentance is a determination of the will, based on
intelligent conviction—sometimes, perhaps, though less
satisfactorily, on overwhelming emotion. It is a conscious
act of an individual, regarded as exercising free and deliberate
choice ; and it belongs at once to the realm of morals and
religion.

How can we do justice simultaneously to this view of
things, and to the doctrine of the New Birth ?

Here I want to pause in the argument to look at some
indisputable facts of pastoral experience. Every one of us is
aware of the seeming impossibility of awakening in many
committed to our charge any awareness of spiritual reality.

This imperviousness to spiritual truth does not grow any less widespread or any less obdurate. We are inclined to agree with the writer—I believe it was Dr. Inge—who maintained that always and everywhere only a minority were religious, and that with most we must be prepared to fail. I do not suppose we readily acquiesced in this verdict. We believed that God has made *all* men for Himself, capable of awaking to their destiny to be His conscious sons, and in that faith we have gone on.

But, after all, was the writer of the Fourth Gospel giving us a more realistic account ? *We* cannot bring to birth ; that we must leave to the activity of the Spirit, who, like the wind, bloweth where He listeth, and then gives His own mysterious and sublime freedom to His progeny.

All this awakens echoes of a controversy I recall meeting when I studied Theology here many years ago, the controversy whether Salvation was *moral* or *metaphysical*. I remember that even then I more or less dimly perceived that salvation could not be adequately set forth in terms purely moral. So much more appeared to be required than a resolve to live a better life. It was not a question just of rehandling the old material : a transformation of essence alone was adequate to human need and the Christian hope. The words of Athanasius had a truer ring. Αὐτὸς γὰρ ἐνηνθρώπησεν ἵνα ἡμεῖς θεοποιηθῶμεν. What precisely is this θεοποίησις ? How are we to set *this* ideal before congregations of ordinary men and women, to confirmation classes of girls and boys ?

The Stoic ideal was to live according to nature. Its meaning depends upon the meaning we give to ' nature '. Such a life, the following of nature, has spontaneity and freedom. If our human nature is essentially changed when we are ' saved ' then the Christian life has all the grace of naturalness. There is, ideally at least, an end to the thought that right action goes ' against the grain ' ; and there comes the possibility that we shall love what God commands, and that the tension between reason and desire or appetite will be done away.

The doctrine of the New Birth implies the creation of a kinship between God and man : for like produces like. The full force of the metaphor is that man's sonship to God does consist in a oneness of nature.

Here there is the sharpest of contrasts with a pronounced trend in many modern works, which so violently stress the ineradicable difference between God and man that one sometimes wonders how God could ever communicate with such beings, and how they could, in any telling sense, be saved. If even the best are so bad, there seems a danger of the distinction between good men and bad fading into insignificance. We can sympathize with the shock administered to faith in human nature and human goodness by the depths of cruelty into which portions of the human race have sunk. But a shock is not always the best preliminary to clear thinking. No analysis of the antagonism between God and man can be acceptable which leaves it impossible fully to accept the creation of man in God's image or the raising of man to divine sonship. The old humanism may have broken down ; the new, true, humanism will be based on man's sonship to God.

In St. Paul's teaching sonship comes by adoption and resurrection. St. John says nothing of adoption : he does not deal in legal terms related to formal status. He moves in a wholly distinct circle of ideas. Where St. John and St. Paul touch is when the latter speaks of the new man.

It would be easy to point out that in stressing the ' over-againstness ' of man and God modern theologians are the inheritors of the tradition of the Hebrew prophets. But as Dr. Vincent Taylor has indicated, the prophets failed in one respect. They taught that all that was needed was that men should repent, reverse their direction. But this did not recognize the radical nature of evil. The sacrificial system touched more deeply the sin of man, by making it clear that something must be done for the removal of guilt. Man must act and God must accept : divine action must be set in motion. The heir of the sacrificial system is sacramental religion.

I turn now to what I venture to describe as the Anglican pattern. There are certain things our Prayer Book takes for granted. The baptized baby is solemnly proclaimed to be regenerate. The phrasing of the baptismal service implies transformation of essence. At baptism the babe enters upon a realm of possibilities that is closed to the unbaptized. Baptism is followed naturally by confirmation, wherein the youth accepts his inheritance, its privileges and responsibilities. Then he goes on to being a communicant. Christ dwells in him, and he in Christ. The whole basis and outlook is Johannine.

The grimmest concern of Anglicanism today is that so often this pattern breaks down. The baptized do not seek confirmation, the confirmed do not become regular communicants. We are on the horns of a dilemma. Either the pattern, the system, is wrong ; or we are failing to work it aright. Or, perhaps, the pattern is not of universal application, and needs to be supplemented to deal with cases never envisaged by those to whom we owe our Prayer Book and the traditions it enshrines. There is no escaping the fact that the greater part of our operations move within the orbit prescribed by the Book of Common Prayer. Our business is to make Christians ; and few of us would claim that we have anything like an adequate measure of success. My own opinion is that we need first to see to it that this pattern is used to the full. What then are we to do ?

(i) The *Theologians* should endeavour to assist us to greater precision on certain points : notably the nature of the New Birth. Then we need a metaphysic of love. God

4

is love. In Him being and activity are one. Can this be
so in us ? and during our earthly life ? We are often told
that while God *is* love, we *have* love. Thus love becomes a
moral term ; and as the New Birth is a birth into love, we
are back again at a salvation which is essentially moral.
The root of our practical problems lies in the realm of
ontology and metaphysics.

Akin to this comes a searching investigation into the
Johannine doctrine in the first Epistle of the impossibility of
sinning because the Divine σπέρμα abides in us. Can this
contention be verified or disproved empirically ? The
scientific temper demands that at least the attempt be made.

(ii) *Pastorally* this involves giving our folk a grander
picture of Christian destiny : insisting that they fall short of
their high calling. It may be that many of us are vague
about the real quality and potentiality of the human
material on which we work.

We need to know also why sacramental grace so often
proves ineffective ; why the baptized child is frequently no
different visibly from the unbaptized ; why the communicant can show no richer quality of fellowship than the
worldling.

This can be summed up by saying that we need to know
what we can do, and where in our impotence we must
leave all to God. Even Jesus confessed impotence—No
man can come unto me except the Father draw him.
This denial of inherent magnetism in Himself is startling
on the lips of Christ ; and is not something for which the
Synoptists prepare us. There is a strain of pessimism in the
Fourth Gospel which needs to be squarely faced. It is the
contretemps to the assurance which declares ' I, if I be
lifted up, will draw all men unto me '.

(iii) Pastoral care and theological conviction must go
hand in hand. It may be that our chief need is not to
know how men feel and think in their several particular

spheres, but to know so clearly through reflection and experience man's essential and universal relationship to God that we can set it forth. What differences between God and man are obliterated by the New Birth ?

(a) God is changeless, men are the victims of change—change in the quality of their life. Cf. the impassibility of God.

(b) Men are transient, God is permanent. Afresh we are feeling the poignancy of transience ; of being as the leaves that fall. The New Birth raises us from this.

(c) God is pure love—our motives are always mixed. Can we hope for this purity in this life ? Will it ever be true of us to say that we *are* love ?

This would mean that *all* our activities became the energizings of a homogeneous οὐσία. Love would thus not be one of a multiplicity of determinations and activities, but the determinant ground of all. Is it into this that we are transmuted ?

Finally—where does repentance enter into the Christian life ? Those born from above are as children—they have much to learn, much to acquire. Repentance is the ever-intensified casting out of all that is inconsistent with our heavenly birth : something that goes with us from our spiritual cradle to our earthly grave ; the condition of all our progress, the activity whereby that which is initially the gift of God becomes our own act, and by becoming our own seals us as free with the perfect freedom.

In the Anglican pattern repentance finds its place both in the Eucharist and in Morning and Evening Prayer. It is not so much the Gateway into the Way of Life but the path itself, and that path winds uphill all the way to the City of our God.[1]

---

[1] The reader can find some suggestions on the relation of the New Birth to other concepts in my book, *The Way of Life. A Study in Christian Ethics* (1946), ch. i.

V

KARL BARTH AND THE FOURTH GOSPEL

by T. H. L. PARKER, B.D.

THE name of Karl Barth is linked, almost inseparably, with the Epistle to the Romans. Was it not with a commentary on this book that he first really appeared before the theological world, presenting a work full of power and brilliance, a work which provoked a bitter and widespread theological war in the nineteen twenties? His association with the Fourth Gospel might at first seem to be irrelevant to his theology or to hold such a small place as to be hardly worth noticing. In fact, however, Barth very early discovered that this Gospel was saying the same thing that he had stressed in a rather different idiom. By the time he had started to write the *Church Dogmatics* it had become one of the chief factors in determining his thought. Statistics are an even more horrid trade than samphire-gathering, but it is instructive to observe that the three books of the Bible referred to most frequently in the ten half-volumes of the *Church Dogmatics* are Romans, about 1470 times, St. John about 1425 and St. Matthew about 1200—and I may mention that no less than 500 of these citations from Romans appear in one volume, on predestination. In other words, it is plain that Barth's mind is considerably occupied with the Fourth Gospel. And I think it will also be clear at the end of this paper that one of the chief Biblical agents in shaping Barth's mature theology has been the Johannine writings.

But to investigate Barth's treatment of the whole of the Fourth Gospel would be a task too long for our present purposes. We shall therefore confine ourselves to his exposition of the Prologue, or more precisely, of John i. 14 considered in its context as the crown of the Prologue.

A few remarks may be passed by way of prolegomena. (1) Barth's exposition is based on a very deliberate exegesis, which sometimes, however, is not stated and must be sought for. (2) It is clear that for Barth the New Testament forms an essential unity. (3) This is a theological exposition. Barth is not a Biblicist—i.e. one who tries to go back behind the development of doctrine in the Church to the 'simple' or 'straightforward' message of the Bible. He interprets Scripture as a twentieth-century theologian, living after the Fathers, the Councils, the Schoolmen, the Reformers, the Enlightenment, the Liberal movement and so on, and not before them all, contemporary with the author. (4) His exposition is noteworthy for its uncompromising strictness. He will not soften or weaken a Scriptural statement because it is shocking or does not fit in. We shall see this especially in the exposition of the word 'flesh'.

In vol. i, part 2 of the *Church Dogmatics* Barth deals at length and in great detail with Christology. One whole section, entitled *Very God and Very Man*, is a sustained exposition, of 40 pages, of John i. 14 : 'ὁ Λόγος σὰρξ ἐγένετο: the Word became flesh'. This, he says, is the central statement of the New Testament, and it ' must guide us in our discussion of the dogmatic statement that Jesus Christ is very God and very man' (p. 132).

The first problem to be elucidated is the identity of the *Logos*. At this point an excursion into the use of the word in Greek philosophy is customary. Here, not even one mention of Philo ! However, let us take heart ; Barth is certainly aware of the existence of the question, as we see from another exposition of the Prologue, in vol. 2, part 2, pp. 102 f. But now he just presents us with the conclusion alone, going for his interpretation to what the rest of the

Prologue says : ' According to the whole context of John
i. 1-12, what is meant by John i. 14 is the Word that was
in the beginning, that was with God and was indeed God
Himself ; by whom all things were made, the sum total of
the life which shines as the light of revelation in man's
darkness. . . . The Logos is He who proclaims God, who
is invisible for all others.   He alone can proclaim Him,
because He is Himself the only-begotten, in the bosom of
the Father ' (p. 132).   The *Logos*, then, is God, ' the one,
only, true, eternal God ' (p. 132).   And although we go
on to make the necessary distinction that He is not the
whole Trinity of Godhead, but the Son of God, ' the only-
begotten of the Father ' (verse 14), we must not dilute the
statement ' the Word was made flesh ' as if something less
than God was made flesh : ' He was made flesh in the entire
fulness of deity '.   The understanding and grasp of this
assertion is vital to our Christology and therefore to our
whole faith.   If ' very God ' is obscured or denied at this
point, all is lost.   ' It is not to be circumvented, forgotten
or disdained in any quarter where there is a duty to speak
correctly about God and about man ' (p. 133).

Four points arise from this :

1. *The Word became flesh.*   (It is better in this context to
forget the passive verb of the A.V.—' was made '—and
follow the R.V.   The Luther Bible also has the active.)
The Word is the acting Subject in the event described here.
He is not ' made ' into flesh, as if He were an object to
whom something happens.   ' In the becoming asserted of
Him He acts ' (p. 134).   This means, says Barth, that the
Incarnation is not a part of the world process as such :
' God's Word becoming a creature must be regarded as a
new creation ' (p. 134).   And therefore he attacks Schleiermacher, following John Scotus Erigena and Duns Scotus,
for the view that the Incarnation is the crown of creation,
the consummation of the communion of man with God

set up at the creation, when man was made in God's image.
Schleiermacher does not reckon with the deadly nature of
the Fall and hence does not see the Word of God as ' the
Subject of the redeeming act ' (p. 135).

2. *The Word became flesh.* The Word is Subject in the
full sense ; He is the free agent becoming flesh at His own
free will. The Incarnation is not to be explained as arising
from a ' necessity in the divine nature '. Nothing within
God compels Him to become man. Nothing at all ? we
may ask. Is He not compelled by His love and mercy
towards fallen mankind ?   ' God so loved the world that
he gave his only begotten Son.'   But we cannot talk of
God being compelled by His love, for He loves in freedom;
not because His nature forces Him to, not from compulsion
to an inner law.   Such a compulsion would be no love at
all ; and, moreover, we should be postulating a dichotomy
in God, a superior being within the Godhead, so that God
would not be God.   But just as God created in the freedom
of His love, so in the same divine freedom of love the Word
became flesh.   This paragraph becomes more pointed when
we realize that it is directed against such theologians as
Origen and Athanasius, who argued that it would have
been unfitting to the divine nature for God to have allowed
what He had created to remain in sin.   God had to become
man just because He was God.   No, says Barth, the Incarnation is an act of divine freedom, a miracle, unforeseen, ' that
which could not be constructed or postulated from the side
either of the world or of God, the work of the love of God
to a world distinct, nay divided from Him, to a creature
which He does not need, which has nothing to offer Him,
to which He owes nothing, which rather is permanently
indebted to Him for everything, which has forfeited its
existence in His eyes ' (p. 136).

3. *The Word became flesh.* The Word is the free, sovereign
Lord not only in His decision to become flesh, but also both

in the act of becoming flesh and in the state of having become flesh. We shall go on later to consider what it meant that the Word became *flesh* : what we are concerned with now is that in all this the Word is the ' free, sovereign Word of God ' (p. 136). Only by the activity of the Word, does the flesh become Word, very man become very God. Without the Word the flesh would not even exist. But without the flesh the Word could and did exist. In the Incarnation the Word did not derive His existence from the flesh that He became, but from God : ' in becoming flesh the Word never ceases to be the Word ' (p. 136). It is on this basis that Barth goes on, in an excursus, to attack ' Jesus-worship '—any doctrine or practice which aims at making the human nature of Jesus its exclusive or even chief object, naming particularly the interest in ' the historical Jesus ' of modern Protestantism and the cult of the Sacred Heart of Jesus.

4. *The Word became flesh.* It is, in a way, a mark of proper understanding of the Incarnation to regard the description of Mary as ' mother of God ' as ' a legitimate expression of christological truth ' (p. 138), as ' sensible, permissible and necessary ' (p. 138). On the one hand it asserts a real birth (' ἐγένετο means quite simply " born " ' (p. 138)). Jesus Christ, through His mother, is a member of the human race. The new man is not a *creatio ex nihilo*. On the other hand it emphasizes the unity of the Incarnate Word : ' He whom Mary bore was not something else, some second thing, in addition to His being God's Son. He who was here born in time is the very same who in eternity is born of the Father ' (p. 138). But in a long and most interesting excursus he refuses the Mariology built up on this *Theotokos*—' Mariology is an excrescence, i.e. a diseased construct of theological thought. Excrescences must be excised ' (p. 139).

So far we have been concerned with the words ὁ Λόγος.

Now the exposition turns to σάρξ—'the Word became *flesh*'.

1. The Word became ' man, true and real man, participating in the same human essence and existence, the same human form and nature, the same historicity that we have ' (p. 147). So that everything that can be predicated of man in his creaturely existence can now also be predicated of the Incarnate Word. In this, revelation is made possible ; for revelation is the activity of God towards men through the sensible existence of the man Jesus. His life was ' the object and theatre of the acts of God ' (p. 147).

2. When we attempt a further definition of ' flesh ', we must begin by saying that what Barth puts forward here ought to be considered quite calmly and reasonably. When he says that ' flesh ' means ' sinful flesh ', we must not jump to the conclusion that he regards our Lord as a sinner, or is lacking in the reverence and devotion due to the Son of God.

' Flesh ' means man in his enmity against God, man as the descendant of Adam and partaker in Adam's sinfulness, man under the wrath and condemnation of God. ' Flesh ' means ' sinful flesh '. And the Word became flesh. God put Himself ' on the side of His own adversary ' (p. 151). This is the miracle of miracles, the ' consummation of God's condescension, this inconceivability which is greater than the inconceivability of the divine majesty and the inconceivability of human darkness put together ' (p. 152). He Himself was not a sinful man, but ' He entered into solidarity and necessary association with our lost existence ' (p. 152). Though innocent, He became guilty with us. Man since the Fall is sinful man. The Word did not become what man was before the Fall, nor hold back and become only partly man. He came ' in the likeness of sinful flesh ' (Rom. viii. 3) ; ' He who knew no sin, God made to be sin for us ' (II Cor. v. 21) ; and, as Barth puts it, ' it can all be summarized in the terrible saying of Gal. iii. 13 : He became a curse for us.' Now, the problems are obvious, but Barth's concern is no less obvious and, we may say, abundantly justified—to preserve without any weakening the humanity of the Incarnate Word, and thus to preserve the reality of revelation and of reconciliation.

But what we have just said must be supplemented by the following. 'Flesh' means the same thing for the Son of God as it does for us ; but the same thing in a different way, in a reversal. We might put it in the form of the General Confession. So far as we are concerned we have to confess that ' we have left undone those things which we ought to have done, And we have done those things which we ought not to have done '. But of the Incarnate Word it must be said that He has done those things which He ought to have done, And He has left undone those things which He ought not to have done. Because it is the Word of God who becomes flesh, the Word in all the ineffable purity and holiness of His Godhood, He sanctifies the flesh that He assumes and remains sinless in the situation of sinfulness. ' Our unholy human existence, assumed and adopted by the Word of God, is a hallowed and therefore a sinless human existence ; in our unholy human existence the eternal Word draws near to us. In the hallowing of our unholy human existence He draws supremely and helpfully near to us ' (p. 156).

But in what does this sinlessness consist ? Not merely in the absence of vice and the presence of virtue, not merely in beauty of character ; but in submitting Himself to the Divine will. Man refuses to admit that he is a sinner, needing to cling entirely to the mercy of God : he wants to save Himself, to be independent. And in this consists his rebellion against God. But the Incarnate Word accepts His position as ' flesh '. In the sinner's place He did not attempt to justify Himself, but accepted the verdict and judgment of God and lived entirely on the mercy and grace of God. And by so doing, He condemned sin in the flesh and made reconciliation.

As a final word on this, we may note that Barth's insistence on ' flesh ' meaning ' sinful flesh ' does not lead him, as we might expect, to holding the possibility that Jesus might have sinned but did not. On the contrary, he joins hands with the orthodox fathers in saying that ' Jesus cannot sin '—*non posse peccare*. ' He who struggled here and won is He who was bound to win, He who when He entered the contest had already won. He really had no awareness of sin ' (pp. 158-9).

The Word became flesh. Last of all we turn to ' became ', to ἐγένετο. In this word stands what Barth in a later section calls *The Miracle of Christmas*. A miracle, because *becoming* is not expected of the Godhead but of the creature. This becomes plain in the Prologue. Of the Word in the bosom of the Father it must be said that He *was* : Ἐν ἀρχῇ ἦν ὁ Λόγος. But thereafter runs a theme of *becoming* : ' all things ἐγένετο by him ' (verse 3) ; ' and without him ἐγένετο nothing which γέγονεν ' (verse 3) ; ' ἐγένετο a man sent from God ' (verse 6) to bear witness ; to those who believed in Him ' gave he power γενέσθαι the sons of God ' (verse 12). In all this, ἐγένετο has to be postulated of the creation, of the mission of the man John and of men becoming what by nature they are not, sons of God. But ὁ Λόγος σὰρξ ἐγένετο ! If we ' think together ' these two concepts of ' the Word ' and ' became ' ' with the strict simultaneity with which they are given us in Scripture ' (p. 160) the event is seen in its character of miracle.

Ἐγένετο denotes an event, the event of the Incarnation of the Word. It denotes also an event that has been completed. Let us take this latter line first. The New Testament tells us that the tone has been fulfilled and the promise has become an accomplished fact ; the Word has become flesh and therefore the reconciliation has been made. And it is an event which is completed once for all, never to be repeated, never to be revoked or reversed : ' God's Son, so the Christian message runs, is now what we are for all time, nay for all eternity' (p. 165). Therefore, since He is at His Father's right hand as the Incarnate Word, we must know Him in His being as a man. ' There is no other form or manifestation in heaven or on earth save the one child in the stable, the one Man on the cross. This is the Word to whom we must hearken, render faith and obedience, cling ever so closely' (pp. 165-6). If we do not know Him in His humanity, we do not know Him at all ; for ' the Word, and therefore God Himself, does not exist for us apart from the human being of Christ' (p. 166).

This is one line that we may take—the ἐγένετο denotes the event in its completedness. But now, says Barth, grave problems arise on this line : chiefly, are we not perhaps submerging the freedom, majesty and glory of God's Word in the flesh He assumed? So let us try the other line possible here : ἐγένετο denotes the event or act which has been completed, the story of the Incarnation as the acts of the Word ; and from this point of view lay greater emphasis on the Word who became flesh than on the flesh which the Word assumed. Hence, along this line we have to put it like this : ' in His human existence, in Christ's birth and cross He, the Word of God, is to be sought and found in His complete transcendence' (p. 168).

These two lines may be followed through subsequent history, as Barth proceeds to do here, and as he did in an earlier section. The former position is pre-eminently that of the Lutherans, and we find it in such famous sayings of Martin Luther as : ' I, Dr. Martin Luther, will know of no other Son of God, except Him who was born of the Virgin Mary and suffered '. But before Luther it is represented by such theologians as Bernard of Clairvaux and Anselm of Canterbury. In its classical patristic form it is, of course, the Alexandrian Christology ; and ultimately, says Barth, is the standpoint of the Johannine writings. The latter position is represented by John Calvin—we remember the fine passage in the *Institutes* which says : ' For the Son of God miraculously descended from heaven, yet in such a manner that he never left heaven ; he chose to be miraculously conceived in the Virgin's womb, to live on earth and to be suspended on the cross ; and yet he never ceased to fill the universe in the same manner as from the beginning ' (*Inst.* II. xiii. 4). This line runs back through the Christology of Antioch to the Synoptics.

We are not concerned now with the historical development of this distinction, but it will be instructive to look in closing at the relationship between the Synoptics and the Fourth Gospel.

There is in the New Testament ' a twofold course of christological confession '. On the one hand we find ' that God's Son is called Jesus of Nazareth ' ; and on the other ' that Jesus of Nazareth is called God's Son ' (p. 15). We can put it more simply by saying that the first line corresponds to the question ' Who is the Son of God ? ' with its answer ' God's Son is called Jesus of Nazareth '. The second line corresponds to the question ' Who is Jesus of Nazareth ? ' with its answer ' Jesus of Nazareth is God's Son '. We can let Barth take over here : ' In the New Testament it is not the rule for the two to be mentioned at the same time or in juxtaposition. On the contrary the christological pronouncements are to be expounded and understood as the expression of either the one or the other of these two insights. Strictly speaking, they cannot be separated and allotted to the various groups of New Testament witness. Nevertheless two types of christological pronouncement do arise from this in the New Testament ' (p. 16). The Johannine writings belong, by and large, to the first type, the Synoptics as a whole to the second. In

St. Paul the two types are equally represented. To illustrate the former we might take John i. 1 and i. 14 together : ' In the beginning was the Word '. But who is this Word ? ' The Word became flesh' Jesus of Nazareth. And the prime example of the latter is the question and confession at Caesarea Philippi : ' Whom do men say that I the Son of Man am ? ' ' Thou art the Christ, the Son of the living God.' Briefly, the general approach of the Fourth Gospel is that the Christ is Jesus ; and that of the Synoptics is that Jesus is the Christ. Between these two there can be no synthesis. They must be held in strict simultaneity.

Now this is the thesis of an early passage in our volume. It is brought up again in the exposition of John i. 14. 'Eγένετο, we learned, can be read either as the completion of the event, so that we fasten our attention on the humanity of the Word of God, or as the event which has been completed, so that we emphasize the transcendence of the Word in His Incarnation. In each side lurk difficulties and dangers which are adequately countered by the other side. Each side expresses an aspect of the truth which must on no account be let slip.

This does not at all sound like the Barth who insists so rigorously on Either/Or, who sees life and theology as composed of choices and decisions and is not afraid to make his choice and stand by it. But one of the qualities which make him a great theologian is that he knows when he must not make a choice. And it is here. Not : *either* very God *or* very man. Not : *either* Logos *or* sarx. But : very God *and* very man. ὁ Λόγος σὰρξ ἐγένετο. It is from the due weight he gives to the three main words in this sentence that the conclusion of his exposition flows : ' Perhaps there can be no resting from the attempt to understand this ἐγένετο. Perhaps there can be no amicable compromise in Evangelical theology as regards the order of merit between these two views. Perhaps if it is to be Evangelical theology at all . . . there always have to be [the two types], not in nice equilibrium, but calling to each other and questioning each other. That is, there must be Lutherans and Reformed : not in the shadow of a unitary theology, but as a twofold theological school—for the sake of the truth about the reality of Jesus Christ, which does not admit of being grasped or conceived by any unitary theology, which will always be the object of all theology, and so perhaps inevitably of a twofold theology—object in the strictest sense of the concept. It may even be that in the unity and variety of the two Evangelical theories in the one Evangelical Church there is reflected no more and no less than the one mystery itself, with which both were once engrossed and will necessarily be engrossed always, the mystery that ὁ λόγος σὰρξ ἐγένετο ᾽ (p. 171).

VI

THE VERB 'ΑΓΑΠΑιΝ IN THE FOURTH GOSPEL

by ERNEST EVANS, D.D.

THE purpose of this paper is to make a very tentative suggestion regarding the meaning, or the second intentions, of the verb ἀγαπᾶν, with special reference to the texts which refer to the disciple whom Jesus loved, and our Lord's threefold interrogation of St. Peter after His resurrection.

The texts which refer to the disciple are these :

xiii. 23. ' Now there was reclining on Jesus' bosom one from among his disciples, one whom Jesus loved.'

This is evidently the origin of the others, for in these we have no longer the indefinite expression ' one from among his disciples ', but ' the disciple ' or ' that disciple '.

xix. 26, at the Cross, ' Jesus then, seeing his mother, and the disciple standing by her whom he loved '.

xxi. 7, at the lakeside, ' Then saith that disciple whom Jesus loved. . . . It is the Lord.'

xxi. 20 refers in set terms to the Supper : ' Peter, having turned about, seeth in their company the disciple whom Jesus loved, the one who also leaned back on his breast at the supper and said, Lord, which is he that betrayeth thee ? '

Here an additional note (verse 24) identifies this disciple with the writer of the Gospel, ' who testifieth of these things and wrote these things '.

On these texts Westcott observes :

On xiii. 23, that the verb ἀγαπᾶν ' marks an acknowledgment of love and not an exclusive enjoyment of love '. This we may interpret (with approval) as meaning that the verb makes no claim that the disciple was in any sense a favourite.

And on xix. 26 : ' The clause is at once an explanation of what follows and a word of thanksgiving : of humility, not of pride '. With most of this we should agree, though perhaps we should prefer to say ' a deduction from what follows ', or a comment on it.

With these texts we must compare xx. 2, where a different verb is used : Mary Magdalene ' runneth therefore and cometh to Simon Peter and to the other disciple whom Jesus loved '—ὃν ἐφίλει ὁ Ἰησοῦς.

Here Westcott comments : ' The word ἐφίλει . . . marks a personal affection . . . both disciples alike are described as objects of the same feeling '. Here, except that the Victorian word ' feeling ' is by no means a satisfactory term, we may to some extent agree. On v. 20, ' For the Father loveth the Son and sheweth him all things ', Westcott has already said, ' φιλεῖν marks personal affection based upon a special relation, and not the general feeling [again that unsatisfactory word] of regard, esteem, consideration (ἀγαπᾶν) which comes from reflection and knowledge. The former feeling [again] answers to nature, the latter to experience and judgment, and so is specially appropriate to spiritual relations.' Here again we may, with some reservations, agree, while regretting that Westcott has not seized upon all the implications of the distinction he has drawn.

At xxi. 15 sqq. we have our Lord's three questions and St. Peter's three answers : first,

' Simon son of John, lovest thou me more than these ? . . . Yea Lord, thou knowest that I love thee.
Here our Lord says ἀγαπᾷς με; and Peter replies φιλῶ σε. In a note here Westcott brings ' more than these ' into connection with xiii. 37, ' I will lay down my life for thy sake ' and with Matt. xxvi. 33, where he suggests that Peter has

claimed for himself the possession of supreme devotion.
Here we may be inclined to agree, though not if the suggestion is that Peter was comparing the others unfavourably
with himself. On Peter's answer Westcott proceeds to say
that he ' does not assume any superiority over others . . .
and he lays claim only to the feeling [again that word] of
natural love . . . of which he could be sure. He does not
venture to say that he has attained to that higher love
($\dot{a}\gamma a\pi\hat{a}\nu$) which was to be the spring of the Christian life.'

Here I shall in due course presume to suggest that Westcott has missed, and to some extent reversed, the point of
our Lord's question and of St. Peter's answer. I suspect
also that he has misunderstood ' thou knowest ', on which
he comments, ' Even when the fact is one of immediate
consciousness he rests his assertion on the Lord's direct
insight ' : for it seems to me more natural, in Greek as in
English, to take these two words as remonstrative, ' as you
are very well aware '.

In the second question and answer our Lord again says
$\dot{a}\gamma a\pi\hat{q}s$ $\mu\epsilon;$ and St. Peter again says, ' Yea Lord, thou
knowest that I love thee, $\sigma\grave{v}$ $o\hat{i}\delta as$ $\ddot{o}\tau\iota$ $\phi\iota\lambda\hat{\omega}$ $\sigma\epsilon$.

On this Westcott says that St. Peter ' still shrinks from
using the loftier word ', and again I shall suggest that we
disagree, for it seems that St. Peter is insisting on his own
word, which he thinks is the stronger or more positive one.

Lastly : ' He saith to him at the third time, Simon
son of John, lovest thou me ? ($\phi\iota\lambda\epsilon\hat{\iota}s$ $\mu\epsilon;$) Peter was
grieved because it was at the third time that he said to
him $\phi\iota\lambda\epsilon\hat{\iota}s$ $\mu\epsilon;$ and he said to him, Lord thou knowest
all things, thou art beginning to know that $\phi\iota\lambda\hat{\omega}$ $\sigma\epsilon$.'

Here Westcott says : ' Just as the idea of comparison was
given up before [i.e. by our Lord's omission of " more than
these " in the second question], so now the idea of the
loftiest love is given up '—which leaves us with the strange
and unacceptable thought that our Lord is satisfied to receive

from a disciple anything short of the very best. Again Westcott says that Peter in his answer ' throws himself wholly on the Lord, upon his absolute knowledge, and upon his special knowledge '. This seems to be an attempt to explain the juxtaposition of πάντα σὺ οἶδας and σὺ γιγνώσκεις : but it disregards the tense of γιγνώσκεις, which does not mean ' knowest ', but ' art coming to know ', or ' art beginning to recognise '.

Now my suggestion about the verb ἀγαπᾶν is that even when it has come to mean ' love ' in some form or other, it retains traces of its original sense and of several others which it had picked up in the course of its history. Certainly it is used in the Septuagint to translate the Hebrew 'aheb, as in ' Thou shalt love the Lord ', ' Thou shalt love thy neighbour ', etc. : and assonance with the Hebrew may have had something to do with the choice of this word, and with the invention by the Seventy of the substantive ἀγάπη. Also in Christian speech and writing the substantive may have had some reflex action on the meaning of the verb. But the original meaning of ἀγαπᾶν is hardly ' love ' at all in any usual sense, but the general satisfaction of a superior with an inferior. Of this Liddell and Scott give several examples. Hence the expression ἀγαπητὸς υἱός for an only son, or (like Hector in the *Iliad*) a son in whom alone his father has complete confidence. So also in Plato, *Protagoras* 328a, ' But if there is anyone who has the advantage of advancing us even a little towards virtue, ἀγαπητόν, we must be content with that ' : and ἀγαπῶ is perfectly good Greek for ' I have no objection '.

Further, we have observed that Westcott regularly describes ἀγαπᾶν as ' feeling '. But I suggest that in truth it is not a matter of feeling or emotion, but of a voluntary act, an act of the will : for only so can it have any validity on the moral plane. I think also that we shall find in the New Testament that this verb, meaning something which for want of a better word we may call affection, also retains traces of these two second intentions, of a deliberate or reasoned act, and of some sort of approval, or satisfaction of one with another, and (frequently enough) of the greater with the less.

I give a few examples :

iii. 35. ' The Father loveth the Son and hath given all things into his hand.'

The speaker here is St. John the Baptist, unless perhaps verses 31 to 36 are a comment by the Evangelist. The idea of paternal approval certainly does not exhaust the meaning, though it is within range : it is a continual fact, and has issued in the delivery of a permanent commission. For the Greek perfect represents a present fact with its roots in a past action.

iii. 16. ' God so loved the world that he gave his only begotten Son.'

Here the two aorists refer to a definite act, which, by inference from the immediately preceding reference to the serpent in the wilderness, must be identified as the act of redemption. It is not that God approved of the world in its present condition (which would have required the present or the imperfect), but that He deliberately set His affection upon it with intent to make it such as He could approve of.

xiv. 31. ' But that the world may know that I love the Father, and that even as the Father enjoined me, so I do, arise, let us go hence.'

Again we have no mere emotion, but a moral act, or a moral attitude, of voluntary acceptance of the Father's Person, issuing in present obedience to a commandment received—a single definite command to perform the act of redemption. Consequently the company may stay no longer in the house, but must go where the redemption is to be made. Evidently the last clause does not stand by itself, but connects closely with what precedes.

Similarly it is by a moral act or decision that men find satisfaction in lower things, e.g. in darkness rather than light, and that certain people (xii. 43), who would have liked to become disciples, ἠγάπησαν, were content with, or made their choice in favour of, the glory of men rather than the glory of God. Also there is a sense in which, without any offence or presumption, the less can 'approve of' the greater : and certainly it is by a moral voluntary act of choice, from which approval of a sort is not absent, that the disciple can love his Lord : so

> xiv. 21. 'He that loveth me shall be loved of my Father, and I will love him and will manifest myself to him ',

where there is a voluntary choice, or even approval, of our Lord by the disciple, and a no less voluntary (certainly not automatic) approval of the disciple by the Father and by our Lord Himself, an approval which is to be so to speak certified or attested by a self-revelation.

I think it is now clear that ἀγαπᾶν signifies not a feeling or an emotion, but a deliberate act of the will : and further, that as the word originally implied the approval of the less by the greater, this sense also survives. For in some manner the disciple who 'loves the Lord' has, with whatever respect and reverence, and certainly without assumption of superiority, found in Christ one who satisfies his needs, one in fact of whom he can approve. I shall suggest that this has some bearing on our Lord's questions to St. Peter.

Now we return to our texts. The 'disciple' passages are easy, and Westcott gives us the clue, 'acknowledgment of love', 'humility, not pride'. Thus these texts will mean not at all that John was claiming to be the favourite, or that he was the disciple whom Jesus loved more than the others, but ' that disciple who is more conscious than the others need to be of the great condescension of Jesus in

taking any notice of him at all '. And we must add that this
turn of phrase, taken in this sense, is more natural, indeed
only natural, if the disciple referred to is himself the writer
of the words. Moreover, Peter, or any other of the disciples, could equally well have referred to himself in the
same terms of personal acknowledgment : but this is
essentially a personal acknowledgment, which no one can
make on another's behalf, so that when (xx. 2) John has to
speak for Peter as well as himself he must use the more
objective word ἐφίλει.

The conversation at the lakeside is more difficult, not so
much to understand as to expound. One may assume that
it has some reference to St. Peter's previous threefold denial :
and perhaps one may surmise that that denial was due in
part, in addition to the shock of a girl's ridicule, to a sort of
disillusionment or disappointment with the circumstances
of the moment. Peter had expected so much : so had they
all : and in the high priest's palace it seemed as if it had
all come to nothing. So I suggest that our Lord's question
ἀγαπᾷς με; means, ' Are you satisfied with me now ? You
are not disappointed in me any more, are you ? ' and that
Peter's answer means, ' Even more than that (ναὶ κύριε, a
strong affirmation), thou knowest ὅτι φιλῶ σε, I have a
positive devotion to you, as you very well know ' (σὺ
οἶδας being remonstrative). So again with the second
question and the second answer : not that Peter shrinks
from accepting the better word, but that he insists on his
own word, which he thinks is the better. But the third
time our Lord accepts Peter's word, and asks φιλεῖς με;
It is not true to the text to say that Jesus said ' lovest ' three
times : He said φιλεῖς only once. So Peter is grieved that
it is only at the third time of asking that Jesus uses the more
positive word φιλεῖς, and again he remonstrates, even more
emphatically, ' All things thou knowest ' πάντα σὺ οἶδας,
and then, with a sort of relief in his mind and voice, σὺ

γιγνώσκεις ' you yourself are now beginning to take knowledge of this positive affection of mine '.

Such is my suggestion for the interpretation of this passage. It at least saves us from the supposition that our Lord
will be content to receive from a disciple anything less than
the very best. There is one objection to it, which may be
fatal, though it would be equally fatal to Westcott's or any
other interpretation which tried to distinguish between
ἀγαπᾶν and φιλεῖν. Presumably this conversation took
place in Syriac, and in the Peshitta version (which is
admittedly a translation from the Greek) the same word for
' love ' occurs all seven times, nor is any clear distinction
made between οἶδας and γιγνώσκεις. Perhaps one might
reply that as in the providence of God the Scriptures have
come down to us in Greek, it may be mistaken self-denial
on our part if we deprive ourselves of anything we can
gain from that most expressive of all languages.

VII

WHO WAS THE DISCIPLE WHOM
JESUS LOVED?

by J. N. SANDERS, M.A.

IN the Fourth Gospel the disciple whom Jesus loved (ὃν ἠγάπα ὁ Ἰησοῦς) is first mentioned explicitly at the Last Supper (xiii. 23). He also appears by the Cross (xix. 26), and finally, in the last chapter (xxi. 20 and 24) he is identified as the writer of the Gospel (ὁ μαρτυρῶν περὶ τούτων, καὶ γράψας ταῦτα). The phraseology of xxi. 24 is clearly meant to echo that of xix. 35, and so to emphasize the identification of the disciple whom Jesus loved with the disciple by the Cross who saw the blood and water issue from Jesus' side.

Moreover, the close association of this disciple with Peter both in xiii and xxi renders it highly probable, in the opinion of most critics, that he is meant to be the other disciple, known to the High Priest, mentioned in xviii. 15 f., where he lets Peter into the High Priest's house, and in xx. 2 ff., where he and Peter find the tomb empty. This is indeed the traditional view.

It may be noted, however, that in xx. 2 the verb is different, and we have ὃν ἐφίλει ὁ Ἰησοῦς. This presents no difficulty to those who think that the Fourth Evangelist makes no distinction in meaning between φιλέω and ἀγαπάω. But if he does deliberately discriminate between them, as certain passages suggest,[1] this lends colour to the suggestion

---

[1] In xi. 5 the Evangelist says of Martha, Mary and Lazarus that Jesus ἠγάπα them, and in xi. 36 makes the Jews say Ἴδε, πῶς ἐφίλει αὐτόν. In xxi. 15-17 there is a subtle interchange of the two verbs in the three questions of Jesus and Peter's three answers to them. Whether or not there is a parallel distinction in Aramaic usage is not, I think, relevant.

that the μαθητὴς ὅν ἠγάπα ὁ Ἰησοῦς was not the same person as the ἄλλος μαθητὴς ὅν ἐφίλει ὁ Ἰησοῦς.

This difference in phraseology is so slight and insignificant that by itself it would be insufficient to justify the attempt to distinguish between the two disciples. The distinction does, however, help to harmonize the evidence at our disposal for answering the question ' Who was the disciple whom Jesus loved ? ' and so I propose to see what consequences follow from accepting it, and suggest without more ado the—admittedly highly speculative—hypothesis that the disciple whom Jesus ἠγάπα was Lazarus, and that the ἄλλος μαθητής, ὅν ἐφίλει, was John, who appears in Papias' preface as the Elder, who had been a disciple of the Lord.

I suggest further that this John may well be the son of the Mary whose house in Jerusalem was the headquarters of the apostolic church, to which Peter went on his release from prison : that he had accompanied Peter to Samaria, and later went with Paul and his own relative Barnabas to Cyprus : and that he finally settled in Ephesus, wrote the three Epistles, published the Fourth Gospel which he had edited from the writings of the disciple whom Jesus ἠγάπα, and wrote the Apocalypse.[1] His publication of the Gospel led to his identification with the disciple whom Jesus ἠγάπα, and prepared for the eventual identification of them both with John the son of Zebedee, which is, to my mind at least, very hard to accept.

He could not, of course, have also written the Second Gospel, a rôle for which he is often cast. But it is not surely a very great strain on our credulity to suppose that there were two men with the surname Mark associated at different periods of his career with Peter. The Second Gospel certainly gives the impression of resting on good

[1] A more likely suggestion is perhaps that the Apocalypse is pseudepigraphical, but was meant to be taken as by John of Ephesus.

tradition but of having been written by one who was not personally familiar with Palestine. Anyone who boggles at two Marks in the first century may be reminded that in Cambridge after the Second World War there were two Ravens, two Burnabys and two Chadwicks in Anglican orders holding College and University posts. Imagine the confusion that will cause to research students in 4,000 A.D.

The identification of the disciple ὃν ἠγάπα ὁ Ἰησοῦς with Lazarus seems to me to be supported by two pieces of evidence within the Gospel itself, and to have been overlooked by conservative scholars because they have been too busy defending the later traditional identification with John the son of Zebedee, and by radical scholars because they do not believe that Lazarus was raised from the dead.

The first point in favour of this hypothesis is the quite explicit statement in John xi. 5, 'Jesus loved (ἠγάπα) Martha and her sister and Lazarus'. The disciple surely must be identifiable—an anonymous witness is not very satisfactory—and here, I think, he is identified.

Secondly there is the belief, mentioned and carefully corrected in xxi. 23, that the disciple was not going to die, a belief natural enough if the disciple was one who had already died once, and been raised from the dead.

The question then naturally arises, How did the identification of the disciple whom Jesus loved with John the son of Zebedee come to be made?

The tradition in its final form ascribed Gospel, Epistles, and Apocalypse to John the son of Zebedee. To accept this involves accounting for the marked differences in both thought and language between the Apocalypse and the other 'Johannine' writings, differences which have induced most modern scholars to reject the tradition on this point, even when they uphold it on the matter of the authorship of the Gospel. It also involves accounting for the differences, less obvious, admittedly, but still to be found, and requiring explanation, between the Gospel and the Epistles. The hypothesis I am offering for consideration does provide some explanation of the peculiar combination of resemblance and difference between the three.

The tradition is consistent with the internal evidence of the Gospel to this extent at least, that in it John the son of Zebedee is not otherwise mentioned by name, and that when the 'sons of Zebedee' *are* mentioned, in xxi. 2, it is on an occasion when the disciple whom Jesus loved was present.[1] But it runs into difficulties, such as :

(*a*) If the disciple was by the Cross (xix. 26, 35), there is an inconsistency with the Synoptic Gospels, which say that the Twelve forsook Jesus and fled.

(*b*) I find it difficult to believe that Jesus would have entrusted his mother to the care of one whom he had called to abandon his own family and accept the vocation of a homeless and wandering preacher.

(*c*) The Fourth Gospel mentions no episode in which John the son of Zebedee has a 'speaking part' or even a mention by name in the Synoptic Gospels. It might be argued that this is deliberate, since the Fourth Gospel is only meant to supplement the Synoptic Gospels. But this plea makes (*a*) and (*b*) more difficult to explain. The silence of the Fourth Gospel is of course more remarkable if it is undesigned.

(*d*) The standpoint of the Fourth Evangelist is not easily compatible with his being a Galilean. The Twelve are by no means prominent in the Fourth Gospel. They come in

---

[1] It is conceivable that οἱ τοῦ Ζεβεδαίου here is an early gloss on the following words καὶ ἄλλοι ἐκ τῶν μαθητῶν αὐτοῦ δύο, and so possibly the earliest evidence for the view that the disciple was John the son of Zebedee. My hypothesis does not, however, depend on the correctness of this surmise.

the Gospel as the Galilean group, mentioned only in vi (which is in any case in Galilee) and in xx. 24, though individual members of the Twelve are mentioned by name. The standpoint of the Evangelist suggests that his home was Judea rather than Galilee. It is Judea, not Galilee, which is Jesus' own country. In iv. 44 the saying that a prophet has no honour in his own country is introduced after Jesus has left Judea for Galilee, whereas in Mark vi. 4 it is applied when Jesus is in Galilee.

(e) If, as the traditional view implies, there is no distinction between the disciple whom Jesus loved and the 'other disciple', a further difficulty arises. Would a Galilean fisherman be 'known to the High Priest'? The suggestion has been made that 'Zebedee and Sons' were purveyors of fish (by appointment) to the High Priest. No doubt the portress would know the fishmonger, but this is not what the Gospel says. The Jews in general were not snobbish about 'trade'—many eminent Rabbis pursued very humble callings—but it does not follow that a Sadducean aristocrat was not. And the improbability is perhaps greater if γνωστός means 'related', and not simply 'known' to the High Priest.

But it is not only with the internal evidence of the Gospel that the final form of the tradition runs into difficulties. It is not wholly compatible with the earliest external evidence either.

One point I do not press—the evidence for the early death of John the son of Zebedee. If this could be proved, it would obviously demolish the traditional case. But the evidence is very slight, and in any case it is not necessary to my hypothesis. Nor do I wish to lay much stress on the Alogi. It is fairly obvious that their scruples about the Gospel and Apocalypse were dogmatic in origin, and their attribution of them to Cerinthus, John's traditional adversary at Ephesus, is quite fantastic, and may almost be taken as evidence for the contrary attribution—like the denial in the 'Leucian' Acts of John that John wrote a Gospel.

The significance of Ignatius is difficult to assess. The evidence of his own writings suggests that he was familiar with St. John's Gospel, yet when he wrote to Ephesus he mentioned the Ephesians' connection with Paul, calling them Παύλου συμμύσται, but saying nothing of John.

Polycarp and Papias furnish us with evidence from Asia Minor in the early second century. Polycarp was bishop of Smyrna at the time of Ignatius' martyrdom, and Papias, bishop of Hierapolis, was his-contemporary ; both had been associated with John of Ephesus. Eusebius (H.E. iii. 39) quotes from Irenaeus that Papias was a hearer of John and companion of Polycarp,[1] and also (H.E. v. 20) quotes Irenaeus' letter to Florinus, in which Irenaeus tells us of his having heard Polycarp speak of his association with John and with others who had seen the Lord.[2] Now comes the crucial question. Whom did Polycarp, and following him Irenaeus, suppose this Ephesian John to have been ? There is no evidence from Polycarp, or, so far as I am aware, from Irenaeus either, which compels us to suppose that he was the son of Zebedee.

If, however, we may appeal to the familiar passage from Papias, he was Papias' 'Elder John'. According to Eusebius, Papias said that he took every opportunity to discover what had been said by the 'elders'—'what was said (Aorist) by Andrew, or by Peter, or by Philip, or by Thomas or James, or by John or Matthew or any other of the disciples of the Lord, and what Aristion and the Elder

---

[1] Ἰωάννου μὲν ἀκουστής, Πολυκάρπου δὲ ἑταῖρος γεγονώς, ἀρχαῖος ἀνήρ.

[2] . . . ὥστε με δύνασθαι εἰπεῖν καὶ τὸν τόπον ἐν ᾧ καθεζόμενος διελέγετο ὁ μακάριος Πολύκαρπος . . . καὶ τὰς διαλέξεις ἃς ἐποιεῖτο πρὸς τὸ πλῆθος, καὶ τὴν κατὰ Ἰωάννου συναναστροφὴν ὡς ἀπήγγελλε, καὶ τὴν μετὰ τῶν λοιπῶν τῶν ἑωρακότων τὸν κύριον.

John, the disciples of the Lord, say (Present) '.[1] It is sometimes said that Papias' language is ambiguous. It is true
that he uses πρεσβύτερος loosely, but the double mention of
John, and the difference between the tenses of the verbs in
the two clauses, are most naturally explained on the assumption that the first time Papias mentions John, in the list of
names, all of which are of members of the Twelve, he
means the son of Zebedee, who was no more (or less) likely
ever to have been in Ephesus than any of the others, and
that the second John, mentioned after Aristion, was a
different person.   The fact that Eusebius thought Papias
meant to distinguish them is no reason for supposing the
contrary.   I conclude then that the John known to Papias
and Polycarp was not the son of Zebedee, but that he was
the John who published the Gospel in Ephesus and wrote the
Epistles. This accords with Eusebius' testimony in the same
section of his history that Papias quoted I John. Polycarp's
Epistle also shows clear traces of I John.

The association of Papias with John is also attested by the
'Anti-Marcionite' preface to the Gospel, in which the
statement that the Gospel was published in John's lifetime
is attributed to Papias, 'John's dear disciple'.[2]

That John published the Gospel in his lifetime is also
stated by Irenaeus and the Muratorian Canon.

Irenaeus, whose Greek text is preserved by Eusebius
(H.E. v. 8), says Ἰωάννης ὁ μαθητής τοῦ κυρίου, ὁ καὶ ἐπὶ
τὸ στῆθος αὐτοῦ ἀναπεσών, καὶ αὐτὸς ἐξέδωκε τὸ Εὐαγγέλιον,
ἐν Ἐφέσῳ τῆς Ἀσίας διατρίβων. He thus identifies John

---

[1] . . . τοὺς τῶν πρεσβυτέρων ἀνέκρινον λόγους. τί Ἀνδρέας ἢ τί
Πέτρος εἶπεν ἢ τί Φίλιππος ἢ τί Θωμᾶς ἢ Ἰάκωβος ἢ τί Ἰωάννης
ἢ Ματθαῖος ἤ τις ἕτερος τῶν τοῦ κυρίου μαθητῶν, ἅ τε Ἀριστίων
καὶ ὁ πρεσβύτερος Ἰωάννης, οἱ τοῦ κυρίου μαθηταί, λέγουσιν.
(H.E. iii. 39.)

[2] Evangelium Johannis manifestatum est ecclesiis a Iohanne adhuc in
corpore constituto sicut Papias nomine Hieropolitanus, discipulus
Iohannis carus . . . rettulit.

of Ephesus with the disciple whom Jesus loved : presumably Polycarp also did this. But Irenaeus never says that John was the son of Zebedee. He usually refers to him as ' the disciple of the Lord ', and his occasional description of him as ' apostle ' does not necessarily imply that he believed him to be the son of Zebedee.

A puzzling feature of Irenaeus' testimony is the discrepancy between his identification of John with the disciple whom Jesus loved and the fairly obvious implication of John xxi. 23 that this disciple was dead when the Gospel was published. It must mean, I imagine, that this identification had been made almost immediately after John's death. If this is felt to be too difficult to be credible, then we are driven to accept the inference that there was no difference between the two disciples in the Gospel such as I have suggested, i.e. that *John* was the disciple whom Jesus loved. Such he may indeed have been, but this still does not make him the son of Zebedee ! On the whole, I do not myself find it inconceivable that after John's death the Church of Ephesus identified him with, and so allowed him to eclipse, the disciple whose work he had published.

The publication of the Gospel in the lifetime of John is also asserted by the Muratorian Canon. This gives a circumstantial account of the origin of the Gospel, according to which it was written by ' John, one of the disciples ' after it had been revealed to ' Andrew, one of the apostles ', that John was to undertake the task. Again it is to be noted that the Canon does not explicitly identify John as the son of Zebedee. Nor does it even call him an apostle.

Polycrates, bishop of Ephesus towards the end of the second century, preserves some curious information about John of Ephesus. Writing to Pope Victor in defence of the Asian method of keeping Easter, he cites the authorities on whom his Church relied. He first mentions ' Philip, one of the twelve Apostles ', and then ' John, who leant on the

Lord's breast, and had been (or " became ") a priest wearing
the *petalon*, and who was both a witness and a teacher '.[1]
That John was, or had been, a Jewish priest, may be no
more than an inference from John xviii. 15, interpreted as
' *related to* the High Priest ' ; but, whether John was of
priestly family, or only thought to be, it is hard to reconcile
with his identification with John the son of Zebedee. And
even if this enigmatic phrase is capable of some other interpretation, it remains surprising, to say the least, that Polycrates, with every inducement to emphasize the authority of
his witnesses, as counterpoises to Peter and Paul, does not
say of John, as he does of Philip, that he was one of the
Twelve, if in fact he believed him to be so.

It may be said that the mention of his intimate association
with the Lord is sufficient : that Polycrates believed, but
did not think it necessary to mention, that John was also
one of the Twelve. Granting for a moment that Polycrates
did think this, I ask if we can therefore rely on his testimony ?
Polycrates claims Philip as one of the Twelve, and mentions
his daughters, two ' who grew old in virginity, and his
other daughter who lived in the Holy Spirit and rests at
Ephesus '.[2] The resemblance to Philip the deacon of Acts
xxi. 8, 9, is curious, and suggests that the local patriotism of
Asia had promoted Philip. It is true that earlier I have
pleaded for two Marks, but I feel that two Philips, each
with a family of virgin and prophetic daughters, is a much
greater strain on our credulity. And if Philip has been
promoted, why not John (which assumes, of course, that
Polycrates *did* think John son of Zebedee, which I question) ?

I believe that the earliest evidence does not support the

---

[1] Ἰωάννης ὁ ἐπὶ τὸ στῆθος τοῦ κυρίου ἀναπεσών, ὃς ἐγενήθη
ἱερεὺς τὸ πέταλον πεφορεκώς, καὶ μάρτυς καὶ διδάσκαλος.
(Eusebius, H.E. v. 24.)

[2] . . . καὶ δύο θυγατέρες αὐτοῦ γεγηρακυῖαι παρθένοι καὶ ἡ ἑτέρα
αὐτοῦ θυγάτηρ ἐν Ἁγίῳ Πνεύματι πολιτευσαμένη ἐν Ἐφέσῳ
ἀναπαύεται. (Eusebius, *loc. cit.*)

identification of John of Ephesus with the son of Zebedee. How then did it come to be made ? I would offer the tentative suggestion that it first arose in Gnostic circles. The Gnostics, misunderstanding the purport of the Gospel, gave it a prompt and warm welcome. With their fondness for august authorities to whom to appeal, and their indifference to historical truth, they drew the inference which it is admittedly possible to draw from John xxi. 2, and identified the author as John the son of Zebedee. When Irenaeus had shown that the Gospel was indeed the sovereign antidote to Gnostic teachings, the Catholic Church in its turn succumbed to the glamour of a great name, and propagated the erroneous attribution. They could find nothing incompatible with it in Irenaeus, though, as I have tried to show, there is nothing in him either which compels us to make the identification.

For the Gnostic origin of the identification, which I admit to be little more than a guess, there is some slight evidence from Origen, though only an argument from silence. Origen usually quotes Heracleon only when he disagrees with him : he himself thought John the son of Zebedee wrote the Gospel, and he does not mention Heracleon's view, which we may perhaps infer from this to have been the same as Origen's.

My suggested answer to this question, who was the beloved disciple, is either (1) that he was John of Ephesus, John son of Mary of Jerusalem, or (2) that he was the person whose writings this John published in Ephesus, and whom John eclipsed.

If the beloved disciple was not John of Ephesus, then he was a Judean friend of Jesus, not one of the Twelve, but a man of the same class as Nicodemus and Joseph of Arimathea. As I have already suggested, he must be intrinsically identifiable. That he is merely an ' ideal figure ' is to me inconceivable. If he is such, if he is, in less polite language, a

6

figment of someone's imagination, it makes the Gospel's solemn claim to eye-witness authority a mere deception, and makes nonsense of the theology of the Incarnation, of the reality and vital importance of the ' flesh ', which it is one of the main concerns of the Gospel to proclaim.

If then it is granted that the beloved disciple was a real person, and further that he was distinct from John of Ephesus, the likeliest candidate is Lazarus. There is no particular reason why he should have been the son of Zebedee, and these are some reasons why he should not.

I am well aware that this hypothesis is incapable of demonstration, but this is true of all answers to this question. All I claim for my suggestion is that it is compatible with such evidence as is relevant to the problem, and that this is more than can be said for the final form of the tradition.

VIII

FAITH AND VISION IN THE FOURTH GOSPEL

by G. L. PHILLIPS, M.A.

THE Fourth Gospel, which makes so many uses of the Greek words for seeing, is also the gospel which states most emphatically that no man has seen God at any time. Yet it is so preoccupied with words of seeing and experiences of seeing that a scheme may be detected, by which the mounting significance of intensity of vision can be shown to culminate in faith, which is here conceived rather as the consummation of an act of illumination, which derives its quality from what it sees, rather than a decision which we make with reference to some external object. The intellectual background of the writer would have saved him from the vulgar error of supposing that anyone could see God with the human eye. Even the gods manifest, in ruler cult and so on, with which the writer would have been familiar, were only conceived of by people of the time, as in some way ' theophanous '. No one would have committed the error of supposing that a physical being could completely be the unknowable and unmentionable godhead which dwelt behind the godlike appearances. This divine essence could only be known in a moment of super-rational and ecstatic vision, quite unlike the ordinary act of seeing, and sharing with it only the use of a similar word, used in a highly analogical sense. This is the heart of the Gnostic idea, and it is most certainly not Christian. It is also quite alien to the pattern of truth revealed in the Fourth Gospel. Throughout, the imagination of the writer can be shown to be visual rather than aural. Miracles of seeing are preferred to miracles of hearing ; God is to be known from an imaginative insight into what he shows and does. It is impossible to make any sense of a saying like ' He that hath seen me

hath seen the Father ' unless we can assume that the first act
of seeing is something very much more than mere visual
receptivity.   Rather, we must assume that in this first act of
faithful insight into the revelation given in this world, there
is also some organic relation to that consummation of faith
in love which will be realized in the age to come.   It is
because they have not heard the voice nor seen the form of
God that the Jews are condemned for not having his word
abiding in them.

It is worth our while, therefore, to take a closer look at
the synonyms in Greek for ' seeing ' as they are used in this
gospel, and to try to distinguish some sort of pattern in their
use.   My suggestion is that there is evidence of real dis-
crimination in the use of the various Greek words and that
their crown and consummation is to be found in the
Johannine word for faith.[1]

The first word, and the lowest on our scale of honour, is
βλέπειν.   It seems to be used emphatically in the sense of
ocular vision, and the highest concentration of examples is
to be found in the healing of the man born blind (ix. 7-25).
At the end the same word is used by the Lord in commenting
on the significance of what has taken place.   The word for
mere ocular awareness is used intensively to point the contrast between itself and spiritual insight.   Its relation with
spiritual insight, a relation of contrast rather than correspondence, is further demonstrated by its use in two places
in the Acts (ix. 8 and xiii. 11) where it describes the state of
St. Paul after the heavenly vision.

The second word is θεωρεῖν.   The meaning of this is ' to

---

[1] Most of the materials were collected at the beginning of this century
by E. A. Abbott in his *Johannine Vocabulary*, to which I should like to
acknowledge my debt.   This work was criticized somewhat severely in
its own day, but we are coming now to a fuller appreciation of its value.
I had written these notes before I came across some observations by
Cullmann in *Early Christian Worship* (S.C.M. 1953) p. 39 ff., where he refers
also to his more detailed studies in French and German on the theme of
seeing and faith.

look with concentration', but not necessarily with a very high perception of the significance of what is contemplated. If we think of the old-fashioned camera, both of these words relate to a seeing like that of the camera, a seeing without understanding. But βλέπειν is of the kind marked 'instantaneous' and θεωρεῖν of the kind marked 'time exposure'.

The third word is ὁρᾶν. There can be little doubt that it has become a word in which the intellectual content of what has been seen has come to dominate the physical act of seeing. The word 'perceive' more adequately represents its meaning for us in English. The intellectual element is paramount. The seeing has become an act of intuitive understanding, of which the classic example is the climax of the resurrection narrative where the other disciple who came first to the sepulchre κὶα εἶδεν καὶ ἐπίστευσεν. The fourth word is θεαόμαι, where the dramatic and symbolic note is dominant. We then come to the fifth word in this rising series. It is πιστεύειν itself. It is well known that the Fourth Gospel never uses the noun form 'faith', but always a verbal form. This can best be understood if faith is seen to be a consummation of many grades of seeing. It is not merely trust, in the frequently canvassed Hebrew sense ; it is equally not a suspension of the intellectual and critical faculty—an interpretation to which the enthusiasm of some early Christian converts laid themselves open, as we can see from the attacks of critics like Celsus. Rather is faith seen to be the consummation of the whole process of seeing and understanding as we know it in ordinary human experience. It is not to be wondered at that when you are given the opportunity to behold the divine glory, there is much more in it than first meets the eye.

It must be freely confessed that in this difficult business of trying to extract significance from the precise meanings of words, we cannot offer complete consistency. Yet it is doubtful if any of us, even the most precise, are always faithful to the rules we lay down in public as our charter. The astonishing thing is to find how very consistent the Fourth Gospel appears to be, and how easily those of us who have grown too familiar with the incantatory language of the Authorised Version can neglect what our Greek Testaments tell us. A simple example of this is afforded by John xvi. 16. Here the rhythmic correspondence of the English can lull us into forgetfulness of the Greek. ' A little while and ye shall not see me, and again a little while and ye shall see me.' The first ' seeing ' is θεωρεῖν, the second ὁρᾶν. The first stresses the note of wondering but uncomprehending regard ; the second implies a higher, though not yet full, degree of understanding of what they will see. The first looks back to Galilee ; the second looks forward to the first day of the week at evening.

The first use of βλέπειν is at i. 29, where John the Baptist ' catches sight of ' Jesus approaching him—a visual awareness which can be seen passing under our very eyes into the prophetic recognition of the Lamb of God. There is a curious example of βλέπειν to describe the Son's awareness of the Father's work at v. 19, which seems to demand a word of more powerful intellectual content. John ix is full of instances (verses 7, 15, 19, 21, 25, 39, and 41). At xi. 9 the word is appropriate to the metaphor of the man walking in light or in darkness, as the case may be. The sense of the spiritual vision is at one remove from the clear picture of verse 9. A particularly vivid use of βλέπειν is to be found at xiii. 22, where the disciples look wth uncomprehending regard upon one another to find the signs of the betrayer. For its use in the resurrection narrative we can wait until we attempt to relate all the words together.

Let us now examine more closely some of the uses of θεωρεῖν and see whether this suggestion of long but limited regard, of concentration without comprehension, is sustained by the evidence of the gospel.

ii. 23. 'Many believed on his name, beholding (θεωροῦντες) his miracles which he did.' Here there can be little doubt that the word carries a powerful tone of condemnation, implying that their attitude was that of those who see and do not understand. For the passage goes on to say that Jesus did not trust himself to them, as if his mere act of seeing men, and specially of seeing the inner significance of their overt actions, was for him a complete revelation of the truth about them. If men were deceivers ever, they could not deceive the Son of Man. In any case he did not require the support of their patronizing interest, but the response of true faith, which the miracles were intended to evoke but not compel.

iv. 19. Here the Samaritan woman supplies a classic instance of the kind of seeing which is not seeing. She says : ' Sir, I see (θεωρῶ) that you are a prophet.' The seeing that she sees has an element of ironic truth about it. But it is, as we say, a dangerous half truth ; an intellectual apprehension, one stage in advance of a mere ocular awareness ; but revealing by its very inadequacy, to us who read it, the infinite layers of significance yet to be disclosed.

Our next example is taken from vi. 2. Here there is some manuscript uncertainty between ἑώρων and ἐθεωροῦν though I hope it will not be taken as special pleading if I suggest that the word I most want is also the word to be preferred. If, in fact, the original word written by the author was ἐθεωροῦν we have here another example of the word used to express uncomprehending gazing, for the crowd followed Christ simply because of the miracles of healing that they had seen. They were even foolish enough to wish to make him a king after their own imaginations.

At vi. 19 we have the word used to describe the disciples ' beholding' (θεωροῦσιν) Jesus walking upon the water.

This seems to suggest that they did not realize that they were intended to recall one whose ' way is in the sea and thy path in the great waters and thy footsteps are not known ' (Ps. lxxvii. 19) ; that they were looking at a greater than Moses who, under divine guidance, would lead his people again through that ' way made in the sea, the path in mighty waters ' (Is. xliii. 16).   Indeed the Mosaic notion is picked up by the ἐγώ εἰμι of the Lord, recalling, to those who see with the eye of faith and not merely with the concentrated gaze of uncomprehending wonder, the name of the Lord in Exod. iii. 14 (ἐγώ εἰμι ὁ ὤν).

The imperfections of this act of ' seeing ' are brought out in their *fear*.   True faith passes into love and perfect love casts out fear.

vi. 40.   ' This is my Father's will, that everyone who beholds (θεωρῶν) the Son and believes on him shall have eternal life.'   Here the sense seems to be, that though ' beholding ' the Son is a necessary preliminary, it is not the whole process.   Earnest, but uncomprehending, regard must pass into *faith* to merit the award of eternal life, and of resurrection on the last day.   This rising scale, from seeing to believing, is illustrated in reverse in xii. 45.   Here Jesus cries aloud as he says—as if to indicate the anguish involved in trying to communicate sublime truth—' He who believes in me, does not only believe in me, but in him who sends me, and he who " sees " me (θεωρῶν) likewise " sees " him who sends me.'   Once again the sense is clearly that no man *really* sees the sender of the Son of Man.   They may see the unseeable in the measure in which they behold him who has been sent, that is, with little or no penetration of significance. This is powerfully brought out by the contrast with *believing*, where faith in the Son *is* possible and so also is faith in the Father who sends.   The possibilities recede from one another into infinite distances, at ever increasing velocities.

xiv. 17 introduces the idea of the 'spirit of truth' which the world cannot 'take' (exactly as we say in modern idiom) because, not having any opportunity of *regarding closely* (θεωρεῖν again) it is not to be expected that it would come to any intellectual understanding of it. 'You, however, *have* at least that opportunity. Very shortly the world's chance of looking at me (even though it may not rise above mere puzzled regard) will cease (θεωρεῖν) but you are going to have at least *that* chance (i.e. after the resurrection) although your seeing (θεωρεῖν again) me then will have a long way to go before it passes into faith, and so on to love and union.'

At xvi. 16 once again the A.V. can charm us into negligence. 'A little while and ye shall no longer see me (θεωρεῖτε) ; and a little while later and ye shall see me (ὄψεσθε).' When we come to discuss examples of ὁρᾶν (always used in this gospel in the future) we shall find that it stands somewhat higher up the scale of understanding than θεωρεῖν. For the moment, let us reflect upon the appropriate choice of these words here. 'Very shortly the chance of looking at me with the eye of wondering and limited comprehension will pass. But very soon after (i.e. after the resurrection) there will be an opportunity for a better kind of " seeing ", a seeing which will mark the passage from intellectual apprehension of significant truths to true faith.'

At xvii. 24 θεωρεῖν is used to express the Saviour's prayer that those whom the Father has given him will 'behold' his glory.

The phrase from the prologue 'we beheld his glory' employs a different word—θεάσθαι—the meaning of which seems to suggest 'beholding as a spectacle', rather in the manner of the Transfiguration. There is no notion that the first act of seeing the glory of the Son will involve a complete insight into his significance ; but the prayer does seem to imply something higher than the self-attribution of the prologue, where the beholding of the glory is hinted at as having been like the experience of sharing in some great and spectacular occasion, the significance of which is capable of infinite unfolding in retrospect. The same word is used in i. 38 of the Lord's seeing of the first two disciples —a vision of dramatic significance if ever there was one— admirably followed by its second use (vi. 5) where the Saviour gazes at the dramatic spectacle of the great multi-tude needing bread to eat, as if in that ' moment de théâtre ' every future eucharistic gathering could be seen. It is the same word which the Lord uses (iv. 35) when he invites the disciples to look at the dramatic significance of the fields white to harvest. How far is the image the whiteness of the eucharistic bread which will feed the multitudes, and how far the more familiar image of the corn to be reaped and gathered ? Finally, at xi. 45, after the raising of Lazarus, many of the Jews, contemplating the dramatic significance of the scene they had witnessed (θεασάμενοι), *believed* on him—a hint here of the way the ' seeing ' words, as they mount the scale, pass into the act of faith.

With the resurrection narratives we arrive at the stretto of this extraordinary fugue, and all the ' seeing ' words chime in, one after another. In order to keep our investi-gation clear, we confine our attention at the moment to θεωρεῖν. This is the word used to describe Peter's puzzled concentration upon the interior of the tomb, and Mary of Magdala's uncomprehending regard of the angels— in both cases at the beginning about as intelligent as the man mentioned in the Epistle (1 John iii. 17) who looks at a needy brother and fails to tumble to his need for help.

So one could go on. Enough has been said to bring out this sense of seeing with concentration devoid of compre-hension—like the tired schoolboy, exposing himself to his books, without really *studying* them, possessing them, or being possessed by them.

The use of ὁρᾶν is confined to the future and the perfect tense ; it is never used in the present.   The perfect (ἑώρακα) seems to describe a situation where there is a finished and completed act of intellectual insight which make a permanent impression.   Here are some well known phrases where this word is used.   i. 18 : ' No man has *seen* God at any time ' ;   i. 34 : ' I have both *seen* and borne witness ' ; and supremely xx. 25 : ' We have *seen* the Lord.'   There is something of passivity and of receptivity in this kind of seeing, as if it were next to impossible not to receive and register the powerful impression made by the object of vision.   It abides with so vivid an impress that it can reproduce itself in ' witness '.   In this regard the most crucial example is at xix. 35 where the one who received the powerful assault on his imaginative vision, of the water and the blood issuing from the pierced body, *bore witness* to what he had seen.

The way in which πιστεύειν is the climax of this series is not only brought out in the resurrection narrative, to which we have already referred, but also in the last recorded dominical words in the original form of the gospel at xx. 29 ' because you have seen me (ἑώρακας) you have believed : blessed are those who though not seeing (ἰδόντες) still make the act of faith '.

The writer concludes with the observation that though he has made this particular schematic system of significant symbols, it would have been possible to construct many others : but the one he offers is adequate enough to face the reader with the same challenge to faith which confronted those who beheld his glory in the days of his flesh.

The biblical scheme of knowledge reveals a rising scale from βλέπειν—to register a visual image, to θεωρεῖν—to look at something with long and fascinated gaze but little

real comprehension. We move upward to θεάομαι—to
look at some dramatic spectacle and in a measure to become
part of it, to be possessed by it, to have elevated experiences,
to share the romantic, immortal longings of the poets, but
to be vague and imprecise about their ultimate significance.
Then to ὁρᾶν, with a strong sense of having ' seen ' something as we see the solution to a mathematical problem, on
to the crown and consummation in πιστεύειν—that
illusive and specifically religious attitude which is a relation
between *persons* and more easily conceived along analogies
of loving human encounter. The modern scale of intellectual certainty inverts this completely. At the lowest it
places faith—a self induced projection of human relationships into a realm of fantasy. Next to this it places insight
—for it is sceptical about the possibility of certain knowledge
in any department of knowledge. It is prepared to take
some note of the romantic satisfactions of aesthetic experience ; but their merit is in the therapeutic value of the
experiences themselves rather than in any truths the experiences may represent. For machinelike registration of
impressions and sensations it accords its highest approval and
puts what should be lowest, in the highest place, regarding
in ' seeing ' all that is human in the seeing as a tiresome
intrusion to be excluded and overcome. When we talk
about ' conversion ' and ' becoming as little children ' we
should not only think of the drunkard rejecting the bottle
or the adoption of an attitude of passive receptivity in
general. We should mean just this—that we must throw
away one measure of what is really true ; and take another.

There is nothing specially modern in this problem. It is
the eternal paradigm of the divine-human encounter.
Mercifully it is not without its analogies in human relationships. All these biblical studies about the question of faith
are becoming more important than ever. The intellectual
world which, especially in philosophy, has ended in an

impasse from which there appears to be no escape, is beginning to take account once more of modes of knowledge
and grounds for certainty, different in kind from those
which hitherto it has been prepared to entertain. It is said,
for instance, that all moral judgments are either empirical
or analytic. Expressed crudely this implies that the prin-
ciples, shall we say, of sexual morality, are not based on any
mysterious sanction of what is right or good (men are
rightly appalled by the difficulties you get into when you
try to yoke these two together) but are based simply on an
actual empirical experience that sexual crime ' does not pay '
and so may, for convenience, be described in the terms of
the old language of the human nursery as ' right ' or
' wrong '.   Or else the assessment is based, if it is to mean
anything at all, upon an analogy to judgment. Which
simply means that you have not really played fair, that you
have already included in your private intellectual universe
(which has, for convenience sake, some similarities to that of
other people) the notion of ' this particular kind of moral conduct in sex matters ' in the general pragmatic concept ' bad ',
' not to be done '.   But this is just your affair and anyone
who likes to, can have fun making up other definitions
and seeing what is included in them by logical implication.

It is becoming clear, however, to moral philosophers, that
this does not give an exhaustive description of human
conduct : and many of them are beginning to discover
something in an elusive notion, which seems to me to have
some useful analogues to the idea of faith, at least to faith in
this mode of vision rather than faith as decision. It is
typified by that situation when we receive a shock ; a shock
at the deepest levels of our self conscious existence, when we
see familiar things, either in isolation or in combination,
in a new way—a way so new that it has about it the quality
of a single and specific experience—and it can issue as a kind
of moral statement which is neither empiric nor merely

analytic, in the rough and ready way I have defined them.

Now the purpose of theological study is to try to think out, and even to present to others, insight into Christian faith in the terms in which people are prepared to listen to them and in concepts and language which they can understand. Here there does seem to be a real point of contact with the intellectual world, as it fumbles its way out of the impasse created by the modern tradition of philosophy, with its rather jackal-like relation to the scientist, or rather its idolatrous conception of the scientist. (In actual practice we are now finding that the ordinary methods of experimental science are much closer to our own attitude—the attitude that is of those who see and believe, than it is to the picture which the older school of theorisers thought was characteristic of the scientific method. There is a real sense in which the scientific method seems to be used by no one, certainly not scientists, but drags out a wraithlike existence in the text books.)

The tendency of those who have most influenced the tradition of human intellection about human behaviour, especially along paths based upon their notions of the methods of the natural sciences, has led to some very odd results. The most obvious example is the attempt of pseudo-scientific psychologizing to reduce the whole of religious belief and practice to projections and substitutions of one kind and another, which, while they may have a therapeutic value, have no relation to actually existing things. This is based, as we all know, upon the similarities in language and the analogies in experience seen to exist in relations between human fathers and sons and alleged relations with divine fathers. It may seem obvious at first sight to suppose that the second, because it is a relationship with a non-empirical world, is an unwarranted projection from the world of concrete human relationships into one of fantasy. Even though there are considerable difficulties in conceiving of this relationship even at the human level and making up one's mind about its quality and status in the scale of human experiences, no one tends to doubt that the correct account has been given and that the ' religious ' experience is the projection of the human.

But religious people give a quite different account of the whole affair, and tend to say exactly the opposite. Their contention is simply that the human relationship, though it is not altogether blameless of the charge of having supplied at least some of the materials for the descriptive language of the divine encounter, far from being the generative principle of that, is in fact itself only a pale reflection in concrete experience of a relationship with something or someone far more real than the earthly parent.

Yet it is a puzzling business to decide why some people look at a common mass of human experience, some confined to this-world relationships, others including alleged relationships with supernatural realities, and come to seemingly opposite conclusions.

What in fact is the nature of the process which leads some of the people to say ' Ah, now I SEE ', and others to say : ' I still see simply what I am looking at, *and I see nothing more.*'

What is the nature of these illusive combination-situations which appear to add up to more than the sum of the parts ? As we are driven, in this limited sphere even of modern moral philosophy, to pay attention to these situations, we shall be enabled to come closer to this strange notion of faith, and so will have direct help in our pastoral concerns when, particularly in dealing with people with a fairly wide range of experience, concrete or derivative, we can say to them : ' Look at all this with us. Look at it steadily. Now what do you see? You still do not see ? Well keep on looking in the *right direction.* Look out for what I have described for you in *words*—poor things I admit—but good enough for you to recognize that what you should be beginning to see, is what I have been seeing all along.'

Christians claim that there is no limit to the range of material which you can contemplate. All alike and every part of what you study, in one way or another, by assertion, or by negation, by yes or by no, will in the end speak to you of God.

What I am laboriously trying to suggest is that when we utter that most common of all conversational platitudes 'Yes, I see ', we are making an unconscious reference to one of the fundamental mysteries of human life, life made in the divine image, and are alternating between the notion of ' being receptive to something from without' (sense 1) and ' seeing the meaning (whatever that may be) of what we receive' (sense 2).

All this will displease Barthians and the English camp followers of the modern school of protestant theology. For I am urging the point that there is something more than a merely verbal analogy between this business of seeing and believing in human intellection, and that specifically religious attitude of seeing which we know as faith. There is in fact a *real* analogy.

We shall not get far in the business of explaining to people what we mean by faith if they have the attitude of Sam Weller, who, when he was asked who there was in the house replied : ' there's a wooden leg in number six ; there's a pair of Hessians in thirteen ; there's two pairs of halves in the commercial ; there's these here painted tops in the snuggery inside the bar ; and five more tops in the coffee-room.'

Men are not their boots only. Though to the philosophical cobbler they give some useful materials for assessing the characters of their owners.

A close attention to this, among many other possible, aspects of the Fourth Gospel, may lead us to a position from which we are better able to help those who are trying to find their own way to faith.

IX

ETERNAL LIFE IN THE FOURTH GOSPEL

by U. E. SIMON, B.D.

IN considering the subject of ' Eternal Life in the Fourth Gospel ' two assumptions about the Gospel itself may perhaps be made without further evidence. First, the Gospel retains, despite its Hellenistic colouring, a Hebraic setting and feeling ; even without necessarily claiming the existence of an Aramaic original the language of the Gospel is expressive of the kind of thought which was current among the Jews of the first century. We are therefore justified in explaining the subject from such a Jewish point of view which is historically given and echoed in the Gospel.

Secondly, we must acknowledge, together with most commentators, that there exists an intimate connection between the conception of the Kingdom of God, as used by the Synoptic Gospels, and that of Eternal Life. Indeed this link is itself the strongest evidence for the Hebraic background of the expression in the Fourth Gospel. ζωὴ αἰώνιος is here not long or lasting life, as the Greek might suggest ; it renders in the LXX and Theodotion the Hebrew compound חַיֵּי עוֹלָם which occurs in Dan. xii. 2.[1] At the time of the New Testament the more common rabbinic formula spoke of חַיֵּי הָעוֹלָם הַבָּא, Aram. עָלְמָה דְאָתֵי, that is, the life of the age to come. It is in this sense that the phrase appears in the Synoptic Gospels ; ' he (the adherent of the Kingdom of God) shall receive now a hundredfold in this time (houses, brethren etc.), and in the

[1] ' Many shall awake to life of eternity ', i.e. the life of the hidden antiquity and future.

world to come eternal life', i.e. life of the New Age (Mk. x. 30). In the Fourth Gospel the position is, however, somewhat different. No one can enter the Kingdom of God without regeneration, and Eternal Life comes with regeneration. Thus in Chapter iii the only references in this Gospel to the Kingdom are followed up by the first passage of many about Eternal Life. This does not mean that we may simply equate Eternal Life with the Kingdom, for they are not identical. But Eternal Life bears the same essential features which are commonly ascribed to the Kingdom. It is given by God, caused by God's Love, to the end that man should not perish but be saved. Moreover, it is a present reality in content but an eschatological reality in the scheme of salvation. חיי העולם הבא happily combines degrees of the eschatological here-and-now as well as there-and-then : Life is present, the Age is to come.

Immediately we notice that the connection with Hebraic feeling is by no means only linguistic. Strikingly the tradition of life as a good and desirable possession is maintained. It is true that the Fourth Gospel repeats the Synoptic logion that ' he that hates his life in this world shall keep it unto life eternal ' (xii. 25), but this sacrificial attitude to living does not imply a hatred of life itself. On the contrary, the Father's commandment is life eternal (xii. 50), for God is himself life. Therefore according to the witness of the Scriptures life is a gift from God. He has set before men a path of life and of death (Deut. xxx. 19) ; but this posits the problem: even a long life is not enduring life. The somewhat Hellenized Qoheleth does not, in Oriental fashion, bemoan life itself, but only the failing of strength, the transitoriness of happiness, the vanity of all endeavours when ' the silver cord snaps and the golden bowl is broken ' (xii. 6). The Fourth Gospel takes it for granted that this is the correct and prevalent attitude to life and death. It rejects all such compromise solutions which propose the length of days and the possession of children as a sufficient consolation for the cessation of life.

Yet the individual's death remains beyond dispute in the Fourth Gospel. Its stark realism again continues in the best tradition of what Cullmann has called the ' pessimistic conception of death ' which rests, however, on the optimistic regard for the living God. The perishability of man, of the flesh, is beyond a doubt true. The whole New Testament reasserts the prophetic axiom that ' all flesh is grass ', and St. John enunciates it with particular theological power. Without the intervention of the good Shepherd the sheep must perish (x. 26-28). Death is not viewed as the natural end to a normal existence but as the enemy in whose clutches is found perdition. The flesh is the weak point. The corpse of Lazarus is thought to have begun ' to stink ' ; obviously decomposition is but the disgusting and observable part of death whose full hostility is not even known upon earth.

St. John appears to argue directly from the fact of death. ' Your fathers . . . died ' (vi. 48, 58) : this is the incontrovertible evidence which testifies to the nothingness of existent religions. The pagan hope certainly does not avail in the Fourth Gospel. The Evangelist, like the Old Testament prophets, does not hold that the spirit of man rises upward, as the escaping breath of the dead may have suggested in Egypt and in Mesopotamia. The Oriental world-view that man is in some measure a fallen god who still remembers Heaven and is animated by a divine spark finds no place in our Gospel. The soul does not return to Heaven after death to live there among the divine stars and to ascend by secret knowledge from zone to zone to reach the last stage of everlasting happiness. Such ideas had certainly found their way into Jewish gnosticism ; R. H. Charles's *Pseudepigrapha* and possibly some of the new material from Qumran indicate that an orthodox Jew could borrow a great deal from the stock of mystical

ascensions. The Evangelist, however, dismisses this hope
with the crushing statement : ' No man has ascended into
Heaven' (iii. 13). The traditional resistance to fertility
rites and resurrections, such as of Tammuz, comes out very
strongly in the writer who despite all controversies still
holds that ' salvation is of the Jews ' (iv. 22) and not from
some hybrid mysticism.

Nevertheless, the writer also departs passionately from
the standpoint of Judaism. It is, of course, a mistake to
think of the Judaism of the time of our Lord as a ' system '
in the sense of a normative canon of belief. The systematiza-
tion came later, as a reaction to Christian claims and
codification. [Honesty should compel every preacher to
abandon the phrase ' The Jews believed . . . the Jews were
committed to this way of life '. Nothing could be further
from the truth.] Some Jews, however, did believe that the
Law of the Covenant was given ' for eternity ' (Ps. lxxxix),
and since it was a law of life some may well have inferred
that the keeping of the Law also brought life eternal,
especially if it involved suffering and a martyr's death.
Devotion to the Scriptures, too, was alleged to secure life :
' Ye search the scriptures, because ye think in them ye have
eternal life ' (v. 39). The Rabbis were said to meet in a
heavenly *Yeshibha* where they could still study the Torah
as in their schools on earth, and for this purpose their souls
were alleged to leave the cemetery from time to time. The
Evangelist dismisses this belief not so much as a pious
illusion but as a moral offence and in the conviction which
immediately recalls St. Paul's denunciation of salvation by
Law. The Torah does not bring Life Eternal.

Even the common and no doubt popular apocalyptic
hope does not find a positive response in our Gospel,
although some of its claims seem to be tacitly accepted.
The phrase in Dan. xii. 2, and the general context of that
chapter had, of course, wrought an immense effect upon

posterity. The martyrs of the Maccabean age were to be rewarded with life, just as their tormentors must receive everlasting contempt. But why only they ? Presently the expectation of a universal vindication and a universal requital found its way into the inter-testamental literature. It is not necessary to postulate a large amount of direct borrowing from Persian and other sources to account for this enthusiasm for a life after death. It certainly was in the air. That ' the souls of the righteous are in the hands of God and that no torment shall touch them ', and ' that the righteous live for ever and in the Lord is their reward ' (Wisd. Sol. iii. 1 ; v. 15) expresses a belief to which not only a Philo [1] but even the strictest Pharisee would happily have assented. But St. John does not endorse this or any other common notion of immortality. He merely reiterates the eschatology of the day : ' the hour comes when all who are in the tombs shall hear his (the Son's) voice and shall come forth ; they that have done good, unto the resurrection of life ; and they that have done ill, unto the resurrection of judgment ' (v. 28, 29).[2] But as against this general judgment at the great assizes the Evangelist holds out Eternal Life. Jesus says : ' If a man keep my word, he shall never taste of death ' (viii. 52).

The Fourth Gospel adheres to the dual eschatology of the Synoptic Gospels and most Jewish apocalyptic thought. There is the ' last day ' ; Jesus says that it is his mission to raise up those who are his on that last day (vi. 39). But at the same time there is a penultimate stage, which seems in point of fact nearer this human plane of existence than the end, and some ' do not taste of death ', though they die, but enjoy life without a break (v. 24, 25). The quickening

[1] G. F. Moore perhaps too lightly dismisses Philo as not typical. He speaks of ἀθανασία, only once of ζωὴ αἰώνιος.

[2] This some commentators find so strange as to postulate an interpolation.

work of the spirit is not confined to the far away future, but ' the words that I have spoken unto you are spirit and are life ' (vi. 63) quite independent of human death ; indeed the flesh profits nothing in this renewal of life by the Spirit. But the Fourth Gospel looks upon the interim stage of life before the Last Day in a unique manner. The usual apocalyptic documents reserve life after death for the heroes and martyrs, following in the tradition of Dan. xii. Thus in the Christian Apocalypse the two resurrections are clearly divided between the vindication of the Saints and the general assizes at the last day. The strong note of judgment also accounts in those circles for the preservation of the identity of individuals. The Teḥiath ha-methim or ἀνάστασις νεκρῶν must be the Resurrection of the Dead who give an account of their deeds. The somewhat strange formulation of the *carnis resurrectio* owes perhaps something to this tendency ; at least Tertullian stresses the juxtaposition of the personal identity of the flesh and forensic responsibility. The Fourth Gospel seems almost opposed to such ideas. Here Eternal Life is also connected with judgment, but it is a judgment which is not decreed subsequently from outside but the sentence of faith given in this life. In the Apocalypses the dead *wait* for the Resurrection (cf. O. Cullmann, ' Wir warten, und die Toten warten '). But for John ζωή is αἰώνιος, if it is true life ; it is already experienced here and now, though death and the Last Day and the ἀνάστασις νεκρῶν lie in the eschatological future. It may be observed how the Evangelist approximates the standpoint of the prophets, as opposed to the apocalyptic writers, in his emphasis on the present, on the Here-and-now. As for St. Paul so for St. John : Now is the time . . . even though there are things which the disciples cannot know or bear ' now ' (xiii. 7 ; xvi. 12).

The data of St. John's eschatology are entirely governed by his Gospel of Jesus Christ. Eternal Life is not a state or a quality of life conceivable apart from the exalted Lord. The knowledge of the living God made the prophets this-worldly; the knowledge of the same true God makes the believers this-worldly because even here they are not debarred from ζωή αἰώνιος. John releases the believers from a purely apocalyptic concept of life because of his interpretation of Jesus. Since Christ is the exalted Lord it would be absurd for his people merely to wait for life in Heaven. On the contrary, Christians 'have passed out of death into life' (v. 24; I John iii. 14) because Jesus also triumphed over death and imparts his life to them. The 'little while' of sorrow, which the disciples endure until Jesus sees them again, does not refer to their death and resurrection but rather to that of the Lord (xvi. 18 ff.). Admittedly the experience of the sorrow of death and the joy of resurrection is still to be shared, in fact, it may be said to belong to the pathos of eternal life, but it is definitely to be experienced in Christ who rose from the dead. Therefore the knowledge of and faith in the living Christ is the gateway to Life and apart from it there is no life. This faith does not only work obedience to the commandments of life and therefore acquits the believer from the judgment of death but it also brings him into a permanent union with the living God. The Gnosis of the Fourth Gospel is not a ladder towards perfection but the concrete knowledge of Jesus, and this knowledge is both love and life and light. The great key concepts of the Fourth Gospel converge together upon that great theme of the union of God and Man of which Eternal Life is but one aspect. In all systems the vision of God had been offered as the *summum bonum* and as the reward of the virtuous and mystical life, but in the Fourth Gospel there are no *epopteis* enjoying *epopteia*, but some men believe in Jesus and thus see God. The vision is corporate; as K. E. Kirk says on xx. 24: 'the experience of the Church makes up for the deficiencies on the part of the individual ; even those who have *not* seen are blessed because they share in the Church's belief'.[1]

This corporateness of life in Christ must not cause us to overlook the new birth of the individual, which coincides with the act of faith. The dialogue with Nicodemus dwells upon the beginning of Eternal Life both as a possibility and as a necessity. The key word ἄνωθεν is intentionally ambiguous, for it denotes not only the birth of a fresh start but also its origin from above. Jesus, the pre-existent Son of the Father, who left Heaven and became incarnate and ascended into Heaven in his perfect humanity, is by the Father's appointment the giver of the new life. Therefore it comes from above, it is a transcendental act and the extension of the work of the incarnation. It is in this connection that St. John's predestinarian doctrine of life appears, as a corrective to a possible misunderstanding that a personal choice is enough to create eternal life. This is not so. The high-priestly prayer considers the authority of Jesus over all flesh to show forth the glory which the Son has with the Father. Only because the Father and the Son come to man from Heaven can man, through faith, grasp this new type of existence. The new man does not prolong an ancient way of life but receives something wholly new, namely a life of mediated glory. R. H. Lightfoot [2] says : ' The Lord did not cease to be with the Father, and therefore in Heaven, while he lived on earth . . . wherever he is, there is Heaven ', and thus eternal life is heavenly life. In the Johannine view, the direct personal relationship between God and man determines the latter's destiny, rather than the more traditional apocalyptic concept of ' the book of life ', in which the names of the faithful are to be found. The predestination is not external but integral to the offer and acceptance of life by faith.

[1] *The Vision of God*, p. 108.
[2] *St. John's Gospel* (1956), p. 132.

Eternal Life is the relationship between God and Man, and opposes every tendency towards a monistic mysticism. Man is not absorbed in God. Even the new man is still the creature under the Creator. Hence the new life must be continually sustained by God and is not lived in its own right. To illustrate the need, not only of the old, but also of the new man St. John uses the ancient themes of the feeding of the hungry. Jesus gives the thirsty water to drink to quench all thirst. He really is greater than our father Jacob, he assures the woman of Samaria, for this water shall become in the thirsty a well of water, springing up unto eternal life (iv. 14). The metaphor of water and of the thirst of the godly is here used with greater emphasis than is common in the vast literature of the background material. Jesus gives the living water of eternal life. Whether the Fourth Gospel alludes here to the mystery of Baptism and the sacramental passing from death to life is a controversial point which cannot be settled here. The beginning of the chapter certainly refers to Jesus who baptizes disciples and this seems naturally to lead up to our passage.

The symbol of the Sacred Banquet also pertains to the Messianic hope and becomes in chapter vi closely linked with Eternal Life, denoting, first and foremost, that the life is contingent upon a continual intercourse with Jesus. There can be little doubt that the whole chapter, with its sad note of bitter controversy, reflects both the Feeding of the Five Thousand and the institution and celebration of the Last Supper. The Bread is from Heaven and, therefore, has an almost cultic significance. But as Dr. C. K. Barrett rightly says : ' The worship of Christianity is an anticipa-tion of the worship of Heaven, but it is not yet the worship of Heaven '.[1] Therefore men, who are not yet in Heaven, must always be sustained, not, of course, mechanically, but

---

[1] *The Gospel According to St. John*, p. 56.

by the living Bread.   The memory of the pilgrimage through the desert of the Exodus lingers in the Evangelist's mind, but the analogy is almost too weak.   Manna, though given by God, not by Moses, by some believed to be stored up in the heavenly treasury, could not prevent death.   This true Bread of the very Self of Jesus, undivided and one in Heaven, ensures not only daily sustenance but the transformation of earthly to heavenly life.

We may regret the fact that the Fourth Gospel is unusually reticent about the nature of our transformation. The anti-Gnostic tendency may have kept all speculative questions and answers well in check.   Thus the fascinating issue of the manner, of ' How are the dead raised ? ', is bypassed in silence.   Even the analogy of the seed, when used in illustration of death and resurrection (' Except a grain of wheat fall into the earth and die . . .' xii. 24), refers only to our Lord's own sacrifice and not, as in I Cor., to the change that comes over mortal man.   The appendix in chapter xxi, too, strikes a very sober note about death. Peter will die and glorify God and John may or may not die before the Lord's return.   In neither case is there any suggestion that Eternal Life is a mythological possession which enables the initiate to be transmuted directly in an assumption to Heaven.

Nevertheless, even the paucity of the material cannot prevent us from asking the vexed and important question whether Eternal Life, viewed as a loving relationship between God and Man which death cannot break, can also accommodate what we on earth call progress.   It is a question which is dictated by considerations which are wholly absent from the Gospel, for it does not know— what we know—the wholly unsatisfactory averageness of most Christians, who are indeed baptized and sustained by the Bread of Life and yet seem to lack the transcendental quality of Eternal Life.   It is a vexed question because it

immediately rouses in us all the pros and cons about
Purgatory and associated difficulties. Another objection is,
of course, that progress involves the existence of time and
that time is opposed to eternity and, therefore, to the whole
conception of the life of God. Most apocalyptic records,
including the Synoptic Gospels, overcome this difficulty
by using the interim state for progressive purgation and
illumination. Consequently the living intercede for the
righteous among the dead, as the evidence shows on the
tombs of the faithful, but only before the final judgment.
The Corinthians' baptism for the dead may also be cited
here as evidence of the identification of the living with the
dead.

At first sight St. John does not seem to have anything
to say on any metamorphosis, ἀπὸ δόξης εἰς δόξαν (to use
the Pauline phrase in II Cor. iii. 18). That there is room
for further revelation, in a general sense, is, however,
positively affirmed : the Spirit of truth shall declare the
things that are to come (xvi. 13) and this may well include
the forbidden question of the ascent of the whole living
man. It is hardly probable that the Evangelist would have
denied that the consummation of Eternal Life requires
further fields of loving service. In chapter xiv Jesus says
that he goes to prepare a place for his friends. The
imagery of space and time is here fully retained : ' where I
am there ye may be also ' (xiv. 3). But, it would appear,
this place is not one : in my Father's house are many
mansions (xiv. 2). Like St. Paul the Evangelist uses the
image of the house in order to bring out the feeling of the
new life beyond the grave. But whereas St. Paul thinks of
the house from Heaven to replace the earthly tabernacle,
St. John accepts the traditional picture of Heaven, divided
into spheres and places where all beings exist in proportion
to their place in creation and redemption. This, according
to chapter xiv, is meant to be a word of comfort and comes

straight out of a belief in God and in Jesus. It is clear that
the Presence of God is not confined to the highest Heaven
only, but that his Presence is already felt consciously in the
lower places of the whole heavenly house. That this house
is the heavenly Temple, where God is worshipped, admits
of no doubt. Whether the μοναὶ πολλαί are stations on the
road to the highest realization of bliss—as many commentators, ancient and modern, assert—or whether such a
semi-Gnostic notion is foreign to our Gospel must remain
open and cannot be conclusively answered apart from the
general context of the Gospel.

This general context, I submit, is not only soteriological
but also cosmological ; in other words, eternal life is a
cosmic principle within God's design. Jesus does not only
save his people from the darkness of perdition by giving
them eternal Life, but he also gives them eternal Life so
that they may share the joys and secrets of the new Age,
of the whole real universe which acknowledges God and
which in God only has meaning. The juxtaposition of
Life and Light is here very significant. God's Life is the
light of men (i. 4) and Jesus is the Light of the cosmos and
he who follows him does not walk in darkness but shall
have the light of life (viii. 12). If light and life are then almost
interchangeable and if God comprehends both life and light
in himself it may be cogently argued that the whole concept
of Eternal Life in the Fourth Gospel implies not only a
gracious radiation from God who is the Light, but also a
progressive realization of that Light. The First Epistle of
St. John, which meditates throughout on the intimate unity
of love, light, and life, declares roundly : ' We shall be like
God for we shall see him even as he is ' (iii. 2), on which
Westcott comments : ' Yes, now are we children, children
with the promise of mature development . . . the Christian
has now, even in the present life, that which carries with it
potentially infinite blessings, but the manifestation of his

sonship is hindered by the circumstances in which he is placed. He will not be anything essentially different hereafter, but he will be what he is now essentially more completely, though in ways wholly beyond our powers of imagination.'

In any case, Eternal Life restores to man the reflection of the glory of God in Christ. This restoration we acclaim not only as a fact of human salvation but as the glorification of the Son, who is the Word of the Father. God glorifies Himself by Eternal Life. The term ζωή αἰώνιος thus fulfils directly the import of חיי עולם : Eternal Life is not a human possession, but the absolute, ontologically real Life-of-the-World-to-come which is the Life of God Himself.

SELECT BIBLIOGRAPHY

[Only items available in English are listed]

B. W. Bacon, *The Fourth Gospel in Research and Debate* (1910).

C. K. Barrett, *The Gospel according to St. John.* An Introduction with Commentary and Notes on the Greek text (1955).

J. H. Bernard, *A Critical and Exegetical Commentary on the Gospel according to St. John* (I.C.C., 2 vols., 1928).

C. F. Burney, *The Aramaic Origin of the Fourth Gospel* (1922).

C. H. Dodd, *The Interpretation of the Fourth Gospel* (1953).

E. C. Hoskins, ed. F. N. Davey, *The Fourth Gospel* (2 vols., 1940).

W. F. Howard, *The Fourth Gospel in Recent Criticism and Interpretation* (1931; edn. 4, revised by C. K. Barrett, 1955).

W. F. Howard, *Christianity according to St. John* (1943).

E. K. Lee, *The Religious Thought of St. John* (1950).

R. H. Lightfoot, ed., C. F. Evans, *St. John's Gsopel.* A Commentary (1956).

H. Odeberg, *The Fourth Gospel interpreted in its relation to Contemporaneous Religious Currents in Palestine and the Hellenistic-Oriental World* (1929).

J. N. Sanders, *The Fourth Gospel in the Early Church.* Its Origin and Influence on Christian Theology up to Irenaeus (1943).

E. F. Scott, *The Fourth Gospel.* Its Purpose and Theology (1906).

R. H. Strachan, *The Fourth Gospel, its Significance and Environment* (1917; edn. 3, revised, 1941).

W. C. van Unnik, ' The Purpose of the Fourth Gospel '. A Paper read at the Congress on ' The Four Gospels in 1957 ' at Oxford, September 1957, in *Studia Evangelica* [Official Proceedings of the Congress in *Texte und Untersuchungen*, forthcoming, 1958].

B. F. Westcott, *The Gospel according to St. John* (2 vols., 1908).